Financing Education

Quentin L. Quade

Financing Education

The Struggle Between
GOVERNMENTAL MONOPOLY AND PARENTAL CONTROL

TRANSACTION PUBLISHERS

New Brunswick (U.S.A.) and London (U.K.)

Library of Congress Catalog Number: 96-17333
ISBN: 1-56000-255-7
Printed in the United States of America

Library of Congress Cataloging-in-Publication Data

Quade, Quentin L.
    Financing education : the struggle between governmental monopoly and parental control / Quentin L. Quade.
        p. cm.
    Includes bibliographical references and index.
    ISBN 1-56000-255-7 (alk. paper)
    1. Education—United States—Finance. 2. School choice—Economic aspects—United States. 3. State aid to education—United States. I. Title.
LB2825.Q24 1996
379.1'222'0973—dc20   96-17333
                                                                  CIP

To Christopher L. Quade

Too Soon Gone, Never Forgotten

Contents

A Preface on Method

It is appropriate to say a bit about method, not just what is done here, but how, as well.

The book that follows is an argument and an interpretation. It argues that America's parents, and citizens generally, are trapped behind unlocked doors when it comes to the question of how best to fund kindergarten through twelfth-grade education. It argues that the key to their captivity is a school funding method that I call educational finance monopoly (EFM); and that the path to freedom is an alternative funding method, school choice without financial penalty.

This argument, in turn, reflects an interpretation of complex educational realities. This interpretation of the nature of America's educational difficulties is submitted to readers for testing, verification, perfection, or rejection. The point is that a primary testing ground for such an interpretation is the experience and thought of readers who have seen the same facts that I see. My interpretation of those facts is what is at issue, and my judgment is that objective observers will confirm the truth of my hypotheses. For reasons best explained in chapters 8, 9, 10, and 11, there are other readers who are likely to experience much more difficulty when they see the argument unfold.

For those readers able to consider this book's contentions objectively—the great majority, no doubt—one of the major challenges will be to learn how thoroughly smoke screens surround these issues. One of the great hurdles to understanding is the effort by defenders of the status quo to establish only statistical evidence as the test for the efficacy of school choice. Thus, for example, the upshot of a recent inquiry by several Harvard School of Education faculty members: "While parents of choice programs liked the programs, researchers found little proof of increased academic achievement. Moreover, the research indicates that choice does not guarantee the program will push public schools to reform" (emphasis added, as reported at a prepublication conference, *Milwaukee Journal Sentinel,* July 15, 1995). Note the key words: *proof* and *guarantee*. Since

there are no true school choice programs operating in the U.S.—
Milwaukee's limited but genuine choice program is scheduled to begin
in September, 1995, and will be the first—there can *be* no "proof" of anything, if statistical comparative "proofs" are the only method we have to
know things. As to "guarantees," again the whole mode of expression is
bizarre, demanding as it does arithmetical certainty for things entirely
unknowable that way.

These words and categories illustrate what in this book is called the
"false evidence trap." Readers are reminded that statistical evidence, while
perfectly attractive and useful, is not the only way we know things. This I
firmly believe: *Never speculate when you can ascertain.* Scientifically
certain knowledge, including statistical knowledge, is the most useful kind
of knowledge we can have. But this I believe with equal firmness: *if the
thing we are concerned about does not yield to simple empirical investi-
gation and verification, then never fail to reflect, think, and logically analyze, drawing rigorously the implications from both our special and our
common knowledge.* Much of what we need to know in order to lead rational and responsible lives does not yield to statistical verification, for
much of what we need to know will not submit to laboratory conditions.
Thus it is that we say, in the terms of one side of the old and tiresome
"social science wars": method must not be permitted to rule subject matter, nor determine what is important and worthy of our attention.

The point of all this for the purposes of this book is straightforward:
much of what follows is, in effect, an invitation to readers to think seriously and anew about things they already know full well. For example,
readers are asked to ponder the generally destructive human results of
monopoly when it develops. Knowing this to be generally true does not
mean we know exactly how it applies to a given problem at a particular
time and place, for example, funding American education in the late twentieth century. But knowing the generally destructive features of monopoly
unfailingly provides us the right question to ask of any monopoly, including educational finance monopoly: why would anyone begin with
the assumption that monopoly in school funding would enhance education? Must we not begin, rather, with the assumption that monopoly should
not be permitted? Our general knowledge of monopolistic tendencies, in
other words, does not tell us it can never conceivably be useful in some
matters at some times, but it *does* tell us the burden of proof *must* be on
the advocates of monopoly, not on the doubters. Recognizing this will

help readers put upright many educational arguments they will find standing exactly on their heads.

Similarly, readers will encounter the idea of "the natural moral contracts of school choice." This is a radically important reality, differentiating a school choice environment from the assignment environments characteristic of educational finance monopoly. The radical difference, and its importance, are well known to any intelligent person, for it simply refers to the fact that, when we *freely* agree to a relationship with others, we thereby create and typically recognize some moral responsibilities flowing from that agreement. By contrast, if we are *forced* into a relationship, we do not recognize similar moral constraints. Indeed, our natural instinct is to break out of such a compulsory environment. These things all readers know from common sense—but they may not have applied that knowledge to education, thereby to see how crucial a role this distinction between free and forced environments can play in America. It can help us greatly to understand, for example, the sharp contrasts between *chosen* and *assigned* schools on such fundamental questions as behavioral peace vs. violence, and parental involvement vs. detachment.

These are but two illustrations of how *general* knowledge can and should be brought to bear on the often hidden (by smoke and illusion) financial underpinnings of American education. That general knowledge can powerfully help establish the right order of things, the burden of proof. Drawing out the implications of things well known is an essential method of this volume—not because I prefer analytic evidence to statistical evidence, but because on the greatest issues of American education, "smoking gun" statistical evidence does not exist and cannot be generated. The subject matter cannot be submitted to arithmetic, laboratory comparison, and testing. One of the primary defenses of the educational status quo is to confine educational discussion to statistical "proofs," for then, absent such proofs—and they will always be absent—we have no ground for fundamental change of financing methods. Readers are invited to join me in rejecting such an artificial limitation, cutting the Gordian knot of "method over subject matter," and recognizing that the decisive virtuous results of parental freedom in education are natural, inevitable, and evident to any viewer whose sight is unobstructed.

1

Introduction

The United States is generally acknowledged to be the world leader in graduate education and related research. There can be little doubt we also lead the world in at least one other aspect of education: the noise level over how best to do it, kindergarten through twelfth grade. One cannot live through a day without hearing of this educational crisis or that, of lost generations in the cities, of violence in the schools, and of a never-ending series of "reforms" needed to confront such issues. These reform efforts promise new and better ways to achieve educational results fitting for the next century, new and better ways to school K-12 youngsters. Sometimes the din—from the cries of alarm, the announcements of new methods, the shouts of failure, and the calls for yet more reforms—is almost deafening.

It is also, in my judgment, very substantially beside the point. For the underlying struggle over American K-12 education has little to do with school arrangements, class sizes, pedagogical forms, and the like. The underlying struggle, rather, has to do with the ways society assigns tax dollars dedicated to education. In the United States, contrary to the practice of other modern democracies, such dollars are assigned entirely by state bureaucratic structures *and* assigned entirely to the state's own schools. That system of tax dollar assignment I refer to as educational finance monopoly, or EFM. In chapter 8, we will look at EFM's historical sources. But whatever the historical reasons for its existence, once such a system is in place, it spawns structures and personnel that work to keep it in place irrespective of its merit or lack thereof, and to keep control of all finances. That is true of monopolies generally, and it is neither deniable nor surprising.

The primary alternative to EFM, at work in various ways in other modern democracies, is parental freedom in education, achieved by programs aimed to provide school choice without financial penalty. In such systems, parents determine the allocation of some or all of education-dedicated tax dollars, and are thus enabled to select schools most suited to their children, according to their best judgment. Under EFM the state's schools are damaged as educational providers because they are sheltered from normal comparative and competitive incentives to excel, to make themselves choiceworthy. And under EFM, independent schools are damaged, often unto death, because they are deprived of the resources that would come their way if parents were free to choose without financial penalty.

Thus, we can summarize as follows the basic conflict that will concern us: on the one side, defenders of educational finance monopoly, the core element of which wants political control for financial advantage, and having such control, henceforth need only *block* efforts to change; on the other side, those who want parents to be free to decide the educational environment for their children, which requires the end of the financial monopoly now preventing it.

The claim that parents' educational rights should equal their responsibilities, and that in such an equivalency lies the greatest likelihood of educational success, does not rest on any utopian presumption of "perfect parents." Rather, it has a minimalist premise: most parents, most of the time, want their child's welfare, including educational welfare. That is sufficient to establish that those parents, including guardians, are more likely to *seek* that welfare than is any bureaucratic, monopolistic assignment system dedicated substantially to its own perpetuation. And in chapter 7 we will show some of the simple, common sense devices that can be employed to help parents choose wisely as they pursue the child's educational betterment.

On the premise that most parents most of the time want the welfare of their children, school choice as a funding policy gives them the means to pursue the end. It makes possible, without financial penalty, an evaluation of alternate educational providers, governmental or independent. EFM, by contrast, provides no such options to parents. EFM is designed as if most parents, most of the time, do not want or are unable to pursue their children's welfare. It is, thus, a *general* system shaped for the *aberrant*. It is as if, instead of quarantining the few stricken, we quarantine all those who are well. That is the imbalance and irrationality of school funding's status quo.

Thus the central point of this book: EFM is fundamentally injurious to children, parents, and the nation; that, accordingly, it is maintained by political defenses of financial interests, not for reasons of educational merit; and that school choice without financial penalty would create better educational conditions and outcomes for those same children and parents and for the general welfare. This conclusion proceeds from examination of three sources of evidence. We need, first, to ponder what we know generally about monopolistic devices compared to free and open ones, and bring these understandings to bear on education. We need, second, to reflect on America's own experiences with educational freedom in areas at least analogous to the K-12 arena, for example, the GI Bill, state-level college tuition grant programs, preschool vouchers, and privately funded independent schools. Third, we need to learn the liberating lessons offered by other modern democracies' great success with school choice. When we have done these things, we will realize that there is educationally no downside to school choice, and we will realize at the same time that today's central educational conflict is not over educational philosophies. It is, rather, a political struggle over the control of educational finance.

En route to these understandings we will identify and answer many of the most crucial questions raised by the ongoing effort to achieve parental choice in education. In what respects are America's educational problems a result of our current school funding method, educational finance monopoly? How might those problems be eased if EFM were replaced by parental choice? If our current educational funding policy is humanly destructive, and school choice clearly superior, why do we not move more easily from the worse to the better? What organizational steps might help this process? What better educational funding policies have been proposed in various states? What can we learn from the vast experience of other nations? From all such vantage points, what can we say about how to find, and then traverse, the paths to parental freedom and school choice?

Talking of "paths" rather than "path to parental freedom and school choice" reflects a powerful fact of American educational life. There are fifty efforts to achieve parental freedom in fifty jurisdictions, and anyone who wants to comment helpfully on how to prosecute the case for choice really needs to know and respect the particularities of the different states. Chapter 12 will show that there are lessons each can learn from the others, but there is no one best way to move from educational finance monopoly (EFM) to parental freedom. Every such movement, while pointing away from monopoly and toward parental allocation of some or all of tax dollars dedicated to education, will need to reflect the special history and political configuration in the particular state in question. That is why various "top-down" choice efforts have been unavailing, perhaps, and why "bottoms-up" is a more likely route to success.

Were all citizens starting from an identical "state of nature" such as noted in the next chapter, with clear vision and in the absence of powerful vested interests seeking to sustain an already existing structure, we could talk rationally about one right path for school choice. That might be no more complicated than saying, for example, our ideal policy consists of:

- deciding how much money society will spend on providing education, aiming at whatever standards society determines, with agreed-upon quality assurances, such as voluntary accreditation;
- counting the number of children to be educated;
- dividing #1 by #2 and placing the resultant sum, along with any special education or low-income supplements, in the hands of parents and guardians who would be told:
- "As the persons most dedicated to the welfare of the children, please use the monies here provided to secure for them the very best education you can find, in the kind of educational environment most compelling to you and most harmonious with your family's values."

Of course, some American readers, so long-suffering under EFM as to think it natural, may consider such a picture "unrealistic," perhaps even daft. For them let me hasten to note that, at its essence, this four-part example is what is done in the actual school choice policies at work in educationally enlightened nations, some of which are described in chapter 6. In this sense, such a four-step North Star as noted here is not unrealistic, not even unusual. If America's parents were intellectually and politically free, and nature could take her course, such an approach is likely what they would adopt.

But we are not in a state of nature. Rather, for educational purposes, Americans exist in fifty quite unnatural states, each with its own peculiarities, histories, and methods of redress. Hence, we write and talk about "paths," not a "path" to parental freedom. There is no one way out, no abstract solution that fits all jurisdictions. The organizational and substantive methods, accordingly, must speak to the particular environment they are striving to change.

In chapter 2 we will look at major symptomatic problems of American K-12 education, and those aspects of the conflict between EFM and school choice which *can* be spoken of generally. We will also show how each of the major symptoms of educational distress brings into existence a "natural constituency" disposed to change the status quo. To the extent the sources of their discontent can be traced to educational finance monopoly, these latent political forces can become the natural constituencies supporting not just change in a general sense, but change from EFM to school choice without financial penalty.

Chapter 3 will explore at greater depth a very special and troubling symptom of our current K-12 funding policy. It will examine the ethical dimension of education; the logical prerequisites for ethical teaching and formation; the growth of social and ethical pluralism in a free society; and the "emptying-out" and disfiguring impact of monolithic school structures on that social and ethical pluralism.

Chapter 4 will establish the causal connections between educational finance monopoly and the previously described major symptoms of America's educational distress. EFM, a *funding* mechanism, not an educational form, brings monopoly's unhappy results to all of America's schools, children, and parents. We will be especially concerned to make plain the *inevitability* of EFM's destructive impacts, and the fact that it harms public schools no less than independent ones, though in very different ways.

Chapter 5 will describe and analyze a powerful and obvious cure for EFM and for EFM's humanly costly symptoms: school choice without financial penalty. Just as educational finance monopoly inevitably brings with it a variety of destructive manifestations, so will the parental freedom provided by school choice automatically fix many of those problems as it dismantles monopoly assignment of tax dollars. We will see that governmental schools—conceived of as educational providers, rather than fortresses protecting economic benefits—will be prime beneficiaries rather than victims of school choice.

Chapter 6 will examine the excellent experiences of various nations with full-fledged school choice policies. The example nations, while not comparable to the United States considered as a whole, are highly analogous and comparable to various *states* of the United States; and it is the states, not the nation, that are the actual locales of American education. This examination can serve many purposes, not the least being simply to establish the fact that, contrary to EFM-defenders' constant assertions that school choice is "radical" and "experimental," there is *vast* worldwide experience with school choice without financial penalty. And it is *great* experience. Beyond the dash of realism we can get by looking beyond our borders, we can also learn much from other nations about how best to shape and implement specific school choice proposals and how to nullify any negative potentials within such policies.

In chapter 7 we will examine several American school choice proposals, developed for particular states. This examination will serve a variety of purposes. First, it will display the conceptual ease with which parental freedom could be provided for here, if it were not politically obstructed. Second, it will show some of the techniques—ranging from dollar and time phase-ins, to local options, to one-city-only efforts—developed by state-level choice advocates to overcome various arguments against school choice and make it politically and financially feasible. Third, we will see some of the detours that beckon school choice workers to leave the main track, such as public school-only choice, and the charter school variant thereof. Finally, we will offer a brief model, and note that, despite the fact that such proposals have no educational downside, they have until now gone down to defeat after defeat.

Chapter 8 will begin the process of identifying the reasons why, despite its great attractiveness, parental freedom *via* school choice has been thwarted and educational finance monopoly has been sustained. The first step in solving this puzzle is to recognize various crucial historical actions, some accidental, some conscious, that planted the seeds of the status quo. Following that, we will take up the phenomenon of "social inertia," that which inclines an inherited policy and its implementing structures to stay in place. Historical events, enveloped and maintained by social inertia—these are vital components of any true political analysis of why we are in the fix we are in.

In chapter 9 we will take the next step to comprehending our political problem. Historical actions and social inertia, vital though they are to EFM's longevity, could not by themselves sustain it, subject as it is to vast criticism. To understand how it has withstood such criticism, and countless efforts to dismantle it, we will need to look closely at the people and organizations dedicated to maintaining the funding status quo. These are the people and organizations—vested interests whose material welfare is tied to the monopoly, or who at least think that is so; and their "altruistic corollaries," people who though not materially dependent on EFM, have been recruited to work with and support EFM's vested interests—who have successfully used social inertia to keep the monopoly vibrant, growing, and very much in the saddle.

Chapter 10 will be devoted to the primary rhetorical tools employed by EFM's supporters as they go about the business of "defending the indefensible." This will lead us to examine the rhetorical arsenal developed by EFM's defenders over the years, and to offer some of the rebuttals of this array of smoke screens.

And in chapter 11 we will point to the political relationships developed over time, especially in state legislatures, which connections have been so decisive in choking off most state efforts until very recently. A particular feature of this chapter, and one taking on great importance beginning in 1995, will be to establish that long-cultivated and long-successful political liaisons, when confined to one traditionally dominant party, can have a dramatic, even revolutionary *downside* for EFM's defenders, if sudden change occurs in political party control of the legislature.

With a clear understanding of why a perverse educational funding policy has been able to sustain itself long after its destructive potentials have been established analytically and experientially, chapter 12 will focus on how to undo it and how to move from the status quo to the happier prospect of school choice without financial penalty. Implicit in what has gone before are the antidotes, and we will discuss the need to reconstruct the political debate on educational funding, to assert the proper relationship between funding means and schooling's ends. A result of such a reconstruction will be to legitimize the concept of school choice for state-level political purposes. We will look at various organizational devices that can facilitate this process, and the political relationships needed finally to bring success. In that connection, we will identify the crucial role of political leadership and its capacity to telescope the stages and length of time otherwise needed to "get there from here." Finally, we will speculate about the "snowball" effect likely to stem from a handful of victories. And, we will speculate about one other thing: how, once Americans have achieved the parental freedom enjoyed by their democratic counterparts around the globe, they are likely to look back on the era of EFM as a bad dream, and wonder why they tolerated for so long such a self-serving and destructive system.

Part I

Symptoms of Educational Distress, and A Primary Cause

2

The Symptoms of America's
Educational Distress

American education, carried on essentially at the state level, is in precarious condition in many jurisdictions. In the major cities, "precarious" has too often given way to "perilous"—perilous for the young people who experience it, for their families, and for their communities. We will look at the symptoms and a primary cause of this distress, but first we need to establish the apparent objectives or ends educational policy should serve in the contemporary United States. Absent that, we have no way to evaluate the alternate policy tools, or means, available to us.

The Natural Ends of Educational Policy

As the great social contractarians—Hobbes, Locke, and Rousseau—knew, there are sometimes powerful reasons for putting ourselves in an imaginary "state of nature." In the present case, it permits us to strip away all the historical accidents that surround questions of American education and the family today, and begin with a fresh and uncluttered view of family, education, and ourselves. One of the reasons we have such difficulty in achieving rationality and justice in education is because, typically, our discussions begin as if, whatever else happens, our first obligation is to preserve the essence of the status quo. We end up captives of and tampering with a destructive system instead of replacing it. We are in a mess, and we have to fight through a great maze before we can even think clearly. Our vision is blurred by long habit, an inertia manipulated by vested interests tied to political power.

Seen from a fresh vantage point, the natural ends and objectives of educational policy will be quite clear. In a democratic society such as our own, those natural ends begin with the welfare of the individual.

11

That is, we want from educational policy the best assurance we can get that the individual capacities of all citizens within society will be developed to the largest extent possible. We want and expect as a corollary the betterment that society itself will experience from the advancement and perfection of each individual within it. As a companion of those two points we hope that the educational system and policies will help produce citizens able to work effectively within the contemporary economy and particularly within the conditions of a highly competitive international economic order. And we want education to contribute to, or at least not detract from, those habits of social civility and good citizenship needed for democracy's relatively consensual politics. Those seem to be the natural objectives of educational policy if we look at it plainly, without any of the clouds that befog it as it exists in fact. As noted above, only if we focus on these *ends* can we rationally assess the alternative *means* thereto.

With such ends in mind we can see as well that there is a natural multiplicity of means, or methods and models of education, that can be used to achieve those ends. Many people can look at the objectives I have just stated and visualize alternative approaches to the achievement of those objectives. That would be true in a state of nature without question. This we know from experience, and we do not have to speculate about it. We know that as a matter of fact in a free society many different people fashion many different modes of achieving educational excellence and these modes are attractive to different segments of society. That is true in the United States, and it is true in every free society around the world, including those far more homogeneous than the United States. As we will see in chapter 6, there is a natural supply of educational alternatives when educational funding methods encourage such developments.

The Family's Responsibility for Child-Nurturing

The next thing to contemplate in our state of nature is, again, logically obvious. We would expect a natural symmetry between what society expects of families in nurturing their children, on the one hand, and what society encourages and provides for on the other hand. We would expect, in other words, because logic would compel us to expect it, that there would be a symmetry in the relationship between family *responsibilities* and family *capacities*.

Barring unfortunate circumstances in which there exists no family structure, we expect the family to nurture children to maturity and independence in all of life's facets. We expect the family to nurture children in terms of their physical requirements, their intellectual growth, their emotional stability, and we expect that family nurturing to occur in the area of the ethical formation of children. This is a particularly critical issue today, where increasing numbers of youth manifest a lack of internalized values or respect for others, and appear to be increasingly bereft of self-restraint, as a frustrated jurist not long ago observed (Milwaukee Circuit Court Judge Ronald S. Goldberger, discussing juvenile offenders who came before him. *Milwaukee Sentinel*, July 7, 1994).

The issue of ethical inadequacy—pedagogical and behavioral—in the public schools forced to operate under monopolistic conditions is of huge importance today. Indeed, though often not articulated in precisely these terms, such inadequacy, as seen from parental and family perspectives, may well be the most fundamental, compelling, and ubiquitous of today's schooling problems. It is a symptom of distress entirely worthy of special treatment in this volume, accordingly, and will be the subject of the next chapter. For present purposes, let us simply note that concern for the ethical capacity of monopoly's schools occupies a central place in any catalog of current educational difficulties. If such inadequacy is traced to EFM, it will provide one of the most powerful reasons for changing educational funding policy, and for enhancing parents' ability to choose their child's school. But there are many other reasons, as we can see from considering the great common complaints about today's education.

Symptoms of Our Distress

There is a general indictment of contemporary American education, conceded essentially by all parties—even by those who are part of the system, perhaps because for them failure is often turned into an argument for more dollars, more personnel, more programs, as is entirely characteristic of a monopolistic system. This general indictment is actually a list of symptoms, the causes of which are rarely noted. And the distress accompanying each symptom has the capacity to give rise to a natural constituency which—if it understands the common source and the fact that there is no educational downside for reform (when the public schools are conceived of as educational providers, not as defenders of vested interests)—can help forge alliances to cure the root cause and liberate the system. But let us look at the standard list of charges against the status quo. First, most urgent and humanly devastating is the crisis in education in the great cities, carrying mammoth personal and social costs. For example, Milwaukee, a favored city in many respects, shows the following: "The percentage of a freshman class graduating four years later has fallen from 79% in 1971 to 44% in 1993" (Susan Mitchell, "Why MPS Doesn't Work - Barriers to Reform in the Milwaukee Public Schools," *Wisconsin Policy Research Institute Report*, January, 1994, vol. 7, no. 1, p. 34).

Second, there is general educational underachievement in the United States. This is less well known, but no less clearly true, as shown routinely by international comparisons. It is nowhere better demonstrated than in a Louis Harris poll conducted for the Committee on Economic Development (CED), the results of which were published in 1992 by CED as *An Assessment of American Education*. CED was aware that there seemed to be large discrepancies in evaluating American education, so they commissioned the Louis Harris organization to conduct a poll of American employers, representatives of higher education, the public, recent high-school graduates and their parents. Only recent high-school grads, not drop-outs, were included in the study, and thus the massive numbers of those who do not even make it out of the system were not represented.

Earlier work had indicated that there was a large gap between students' impression of the quality of their education and the judgments of those who want to hire or further educate these young people. The CED-Harris study was designed to test that gap. The results are devastating and should be a wake-up call for any parents who think graduation alone signifies satisfactory achievement. Regarding that too-rosy inclination, American Federation of Teachers (AFT) President Albert Shanker says the study "is the story of two different worlds: the fantasy land of American students and their parents who think they're tops in education performance and the real world of educators and employers who say our high school graduates can't cut it in college and on the job. We therefore have a choice: allow our youngsters to continue to live in a fantasy world which does not issue paychecks, or insist that they meet higher standards and work harder at school today so they can make it in the real world tomorrow" (back-page commentary from *An Assessment of American Education*).

Of course, Shanker's prescription is always the same: more money for public schools and teachers, even though hugely increased budgets in the last two decades have not been accompanied by improved educational achievement; no link has been found between educational expenditure and educational quality; and despite the fact that international comparisons show we are already spending more per pupil than all other nations except Switzerland (see, e.g., Janet Novack, "What Do We Get For Our School Dollars?" *Forbes*, October 12, 1992, pp. 92–96; and "Education at a Glance," a December, 1993, report on comparative expenditures by the Organization for Economic Cooperation and Development [OECD]). But though Shanker does not know the solution—educational choice—he surely interprets the Harris results correctly. For example, while 70 percent of graduates and 71 percent of their parents think they were "learning mathematics well," only 27 percent of college educators shared that judgment; as to "learning how to write well" the same comparisons were 71 percent, 77 percent, and 18 percent; while for "learning how to solve complex problems" they were 63 percent, 71 percent, and 15 percent (p. 10 of *An Assessment of American Education*). Lest we think educators were simply using unrealistic standards, let us note that employers evaluated the recent grads even more harshly on the same three qualities: 22 percent gave positive responses regarding math skills, while 74 percent gave negative; on writing well, 12 percent positive and 84 percent negative; on solving complex problems, 10 percent positive and 86 percent negative (p. 8).

These startling disparities illustrate the reality that America's educational achievement problems are not confined to the crises besetting the central cities. By standard international comparisons and by the assessment of all who "consume" our educational "products," the system in general is underperforming. That students and parents do not know it does not change the fact, and probably derives from the very absence of comparison and competition typical of a monopolistic environment.

The third point in the indictment is that despite the poor performance, educational costs have been escalating rapidly, but there is no apparent connection of cost to educational outcome. This escalation in costs represents a great burden on the taxpayer, especially property owners in most American jurisdictions, and on the whole economy. For example, according to the National Center for Education Statistics' January, 1993, report, United States per-pupil expenditure in constant 1989–90 dollars rose from approximately $3,000 in 1970 to approximately $5,000 in 1990 (*120 Years of American Education: A Statistical Portrait*, Thomas D. Snyder, ed., National Center for Education Statistics, United States Department of Education, Office of Educational Research and Improvement, p. 33). This is to be considered alongside Eric A. Hanushek's conclusion in his ongoing study of the effects of increased expenditures on school performance: "Over the past quarter century researchers have made the surprising discovery that there is little systematic relationship between school resources and student performance" ("Making America's Schools Work, This Time Money is Not the Answer," *The Brookings Review*, Fall, 1994, p. 10).

The fourth item on the bill of particulars in a true analysis of the nation's educational system is cost's companion: the program, personnel, and bureaucratic proliferation so unsettling to anyone concerned about too much governmental presence in society generally and in the educational arena particularly. These proliferating tentacles, dedicated to maintaining the finance monopoly, wrap around the exposed power points of American politics to perpetuate themselves and the system from which they draw their disproportionate sustenance. According to the 1993 Organization for Economic Cooperation and Development's (OECD) study noted above, 5.6 percent of American workers are employed in education, and 2.6 percent actually teach. The remaining 3 percent consist of support staff and administrators, essentially nonacademic personnel. Among OECD nations, only in America does nonteaching staff outnumber teachers.

The fifth symptom is that the public schools, operating behind the immunizing protections of finance monopoly, are beyond the control of the parent consumers and effectively outside all normal dialectical restraints. As a result, they do not reflect parental desires directly and not even indirectly *via* political responsibility.

The directly related and last of the particular indictments, noted above and discussed at length in the next chapter, is that the public schools that operate within the finance monopoly have become less and less capable of serving American families as ethical extensions of themselves, to teach ethics and demand ethical behavior. Indeed, they have too often become centers of counter-family values in a kind of culture war.

These sad symptoms of educational failure lead to the creation of corollary groups demanding change and improvement. Though smoke screens may at first stop them from seeing the real route to improvement, these groups are, nonetheless, the "natural constituencies of school choice." For school choice, once understood, will be seen by them as a basic solution to their most aggravating educational problems. Major constituency groups include:

- parents generally, witnessing educational underachievement, are a primary and ultimately decisive constituency;
- and parents of the critically endangered children of the inner cities, parents who know education can be a way out for their youngsters, but who see persisting failure instead;
- and the business community, intensely concerned for a well-schooled work force able to help America be competitive in the new world;
- and the taxpayers' associations seeing ever-rising school costs without educational betterment;
- and the burgeoning numbers of people who realize and abhor the fact that current educational finance methods have created massive monopolistic bureaucratic structures in all states and districts;
- finally, the large and growing number of parents and citizens who want their children to be in schools that support, or at least do not undermine, the values taught at home. The tremendous growth of home schooling in recent years, despite its great demands on parents' time and effort, is a dramatic indicator of this concern.

These are school choice's natural constituencies. Sensitized, organized, and related to the political process, they have sufficient political mass to break the monopoly and replace it with parental freedom, school choice without financial penalty. However, for the most part, that growth of political consciousness and spirit of coalition has not occurred. Until recently, in most jurisdictions, these natural constituencies of school choice have been "hanging alone" rather than together; they have permitted their energies to be co-opted by so-called reforms *within* the system of EFM rather than insisting on reforms *of* it; and they have been blinded by the many smoke screens employed by defenders of the status quo. To the extent that describes reality, it also tells us what needs to be done to bring about basic reform.

3

A Special and Definitive Symptom

The central proposition of this chapter is that, in the United States, the educational finance monopoly (EFM) besetting us contributes directly to an ethic of the lowest common denominator, then to ethical relativism, and finally to a moral vacuum in the educational environment fostered by the monopoly's schools. And such vacuums tend to be filled by transient secular trends, thought legitimate by some because not religiously derived, but clearly as value-laden as any religious creed.

Because of educational finance monopoly, most American students, nearly 90 percent of them, are economically forced by it to attend state-provided public schools (for ethical purposes, peas-in-a-pod public schools). This sets in place several dynamics that contribute to ethical relativism. First, there is a correct and virtuous realization that if you force people of many different types into a common circumstance, and remain liberal and humane in your view of them, then you should not impose on them someone else's values. I am not here referring to simple civic virtues—"It is good to vote"—that society may well urge be commonly observed to help protect the social fabric. I am talking about particular values, often religiously derived and family-inculcated—the *family's* values, as contrasted with the generic concept of *family values*. Liberal and humane attitudes clearly say: do not impose such values on the unsuspecting. Thus there is, in a common school framework set within a greatly pluralistic society, a righteous reason to avoid imposing partial, specific, and rigorous values on captive audiences. The problem with that virtuous avoidance, however, is that it results in an inevitable if unintended void, a kind of vacuum. Specific rules of conduct and guidance, germane to youngsters' upbringing, tend not to be propounded.

Second, in the United States this problem is greatly aggravated by the fact that many of the concrete solutions to vexing issues about what can

and cannot be taught have been arrived at by judicial fiat rather than legislative give and take, even though in the latter, prudent compromises
have a better chance of success. As a result, the common public schools
increasingly have been closed to any expression of religious value, as
individual claims have been permitted to drown out majority and community interests. "Don't make my son pray in public school" becomes
"no prayer can be offered in public schools, not even voluntary ones."
Such policy excesses in the United States, rooted as they are in the uniquely
overextended American practice of judicial review, wherein courts become surrogate and innately defective legislatures, are less likely to develop in Europe, for example.

In describing the inadequacy of ethical teaching and guidance in
American education, I am not talking about good guys and bad guys, or
character defects. I am not talking about public school teachers or administrators being less ethically sensitive than other people. I am talking
rather about structures and policies that make it difficult or impossible
for even "good guys" with sterling character to be effective ethical teachers and guides because of the underlying arrangements that give tone
and direction to American educational experiences. The previously
mentioned president of the American Federation of Teachers, Albert
Shanker, a tireless defender of the finance monopoly from which his
members benefit, tried to defend their ethical capability and, in so doing, perfectly described the inadequacy they confront. He said AFT
members "have always been strong proponents of teaching and of mod-
eling *universally* accepted values in our schools" (*The Wall Street Journal*, September 18, 1991, emphasis added.) In a modern, free, pluralistic
society, universally held values are few, they are generic, and they do
not provide a firm basis for rigorous ethical guidance. In the American
context, then, I would describe educational choice without financial
penalty as a *cure* for ethical deficiencies in K-12 education. It would be
a cure because it would enable parents with particular ethical views to
seek out schools compatible with those views; and because, if the public schools saw an exodus for such reasons, we can assume they would
work harder to reestablish their own ethical capacity and credibility by
opposing today's often bizarre policies. If we were in a state of nature,
by contrast with our real situation in late-twentieth century America,
educational choice could be thought of as *preventive medicine* to insure that unintended ethical relativizing would never occur.

Three Fundamental Realities

There are three foundation stones underpinning my contention that educational finance monopoly encourages an ethical void and educational choice without financial penalty can help cure or prevent it. The first is my understanding of how we do ethics at all, how we do ethical reflection, and how we do ethical instruction and guidance for the young. Purely empirically, I observe that the whole of life is a life of choosing, differentiating among optional actions precisely on value grounds. This seems to me to be the central characteristic of human existence as contrasted with any other life form with which we are familiar. We see things in terms of ought and ought not, and aim to "do good and avoid evil," as Aquinas said. We will not act effectively on that inclination, and rigorously distinguish among things in terms of ought and ought not without solid and specific ethical norms and starting places. It is not true that we do ethics in general. We do ethics in specifics. "General ethical disposition" is rather like C.S. Lewis' description of general or "mere" Christianity: it is "a hall out of which doors open into several rooms." Getting to the hall is vital, crucial—but insufficient, for "it is in the rooms [the specific credal churches], not in the hall, that there are fires and chairs and meals" (*Mere Christianity*, 1952 edition, New York, Macmillan, p. 12).

So with ethics: while we can, even must, recognize the general nature of man as a valuing creature, when we want to talk about, evaluate, and recommend ethical behavior we call upon specific norms from specific ethical sources, religious or otherwise. These sources provide the sanctions for the norms. "Who says so?" is more than a childish question.

Such are the norms to which we call people back when we judge them to be erring in their behavior. But though serious ethical evaluation and admonition require specific, shared ethical foundations from which to operate, that does not mean that those ethical foundations and specifics have to be socially divisive or disruptive. American Catholic schools, for example, while sharply distinguished from public ones by deep religious roots, have consistently produced citizens at least as dedicated to the common good as any other social group, and that is not surprising. To begin with, we legitimately surround the different ethical communities in society with the demands and expectations of social order and reminders that the jungle is social order's alternative, thus limiting any disruptive potential such communities might have. But quite apart from that, most major ethical systems, religious and philosophical, have benevolence close to their core. Certainly that is true in the Judeo-Christian traditions. Moreover, much of the most powerful argumentation for natural law rests on the fact that, though starting from greatly different places, men and communities often converge at the point of policy and practical judgment (see, e.g., Jacques Maritain, *Man and the State*, Chicago, 1951, chapter IV, pp. 76ff.). We realize, thus, that though ethics requires specific starting points, that need not mean warfare. It simply means that we do not stand on general grounds, but on particular ones, when we begin our ethical choosing and teaching. If we do not have those kinds of relatively vital and special ethical beginnings, then we tend either to have a vacuum of ethical perception, or the vacuum is filled by the imposition of someone else's ethical views as if they were universally accepted. And that, it seems to me, is the natural tendency of common schools protected by monopoly financing in free and multiplistic societies.

The second bedrock on which my core contention rests is that we naturally expect families to provide the first and crucial nurturing for the child, and such nurturing is expected to attend to intellectual and moral formation as well as the child's physical needs. Please note that I am talking about *moral* expectations we have for family responsibilities extending to all forms of nurturing. I am not pretending such expectations are always fulfilled, of course. But our social and political structure *expects* family nurturing of children, and thus should encourage it. If that is true, then there is also a natural desire, even expectation, that the educational environment into which the young will proceed will be compatible with the family value structures that the youngsters have already experienced. I say compatible, meaning neutral at the worst, supportive at the best, but in any case not at war with or subverting the family's value structure. For if the schools undermine the family's ethical framework, they are weakening basic family authority and moral credibility, and the self-restraints and positive directions the youngster can draw from pride in and respect for his family. *A child whose education, intentionally or otherwise, seriously diminishes the moral credibility of a loving family is, in effect, being cut adrift with no compass, and no ethical North Star.*

The truth and pertinence of this judgment does not depend on all families being loving, as I noted previously. It is enough that most families, most of the time, want moral formation to occur, and want it to be in harmony with values articulated in the home. And, reflecting this, it is clearly true that American society has never consciously chosen to supplant home and family as the foundation of moral formation. We are here talking about the ideal or end toward which public policy is directed. If we want greater family unity and integrity, then policy should encourage it, not discourage it by driving wedges between home and school.

Ultimately, of course, the values proffered by the family must be affirmed, or perfected, or perhaps even rejected by the youngster as that youngster matures and takes on his own identity. I am not talking, in other words, about imprisoning children in value structures imposed upon them by their parents in some rigid, and prisonlike fashion. As I often say, the child is free—but the parents are not! The parents are obliged to make a moral offering to their children, which offering will be sorely missed if not present. They would be very poor parents, indeed, who did not see their responsibilities to encourage a sense of the ought and the ought not, and to inform that sense with specific moral guidelines from their own experiences and most profound convictions. And the point is not to turn the youngster into an automaton, but to fill out one of the crucial aspects of that youngster's development. By contrast, schools formed to reflect a nonexistent and illusory universality, such as those that grow up behind an educational finance monopoly, disrupt the family's natural desire and responsibility to provide a nurturing ethical context for the child's education. (For fuller discussion of this key issue, see my "The Family's Values and Educational Choice," *The Family in America*, vol. 7, no. 3, March, 1993).

And the third basis for this chapter's central proposition is that democracy as a political form naturally gives rise to social pluralism, which pluralism will reflect the multiple values and value-systems evolved by free peoples. That freedom is a virtue to be cherished, obviously. But it also has certain negative potentials, or traps, that must be understood for political and educational purposes. If, for example, democracy's natural tendency to invite pluralism causes us to support only common places, because we do not want one group's values imposed upon other groups, then in these common places there will be no sharp values, only generic ones. If cultural pluralism is a fact, and at the same time we insist on common structures only, there will be a void likely to be filled by secular trends reflected in prevailing law or opinion-leading media. This is the process which, in the United States, has led to school-based efforts to declare "normal" certain behavioral patterns judged abnormal and aberrant by most parents. Or, if we insist on only common structures, and there is a dominant element within our pluralistic society, we may end up with imposition. That is exemplified by American experience in which the Protestant ethic in the last century was quite thoroughly adopted in the common structure of public schools. This was repugnant to American Catholics, and helped prompt the separate American Catholic system. The nuns gave American Catholics educational choice without serious financial penalty, but the system they created is now under drastic strain from the finance monopoly that surrounds the public structure from which the Catholics were alienated.

The second trap that flows from democracy's natural encouragement of pluralism, and which has direct pertinence to educational policy questions, is that if we permit pluralism to be transformed from being the natural *result* of democracy into being an *objective* of democracy, then we in fact are calling upon ourselves to relativize our values, because we are saying that we who stand for specific things should not just tolerate but *promote* other things contrary to our own principles. That has a necessarily relativizing influence on our own values. It is an emptying out that really needs to be avoided at all costs. Both these traps are wrong responses to the social and ethical pluralism that democracy naturally nourishes. Tolerance and benevolence are the best we can offer those with whom we differ, if we seriously hold serious values. (For more on this, please see my "Pluralism *vs.* Diversity," *Freedom Review*, vol. 22, no. 2, 1991, and *Current*, No. 334, July-August, 1991.)

Forcing Only Common Schools on a Pluralist Society

These are the reasons that make it clear to me that the choice of educational finance policy—finance monopoly, on the one hand, vs. parental allocation and choice on the other—impacts directly on the ethical strength and sensitivities that a society can be expected to manifest. The prevailing conditions in the United States, reflecting not ethical inadequacies of personnel, but the very often unintended effects of injurious structures and policies, are in fact contributing to a kind of ethical juvenility, egocentrism, and lack of self-restraint on the part of American youth. Because of the unfolding logic of educational finance monopoly in a modern pluralistic society, those young people are cut off in substantial part from the natural progression of ethical nurturing, teaching, and guidance that can occur when schooling proceeds from, or is at least compatible with, the home and family. As will be seen more fully in subsequent chapters, educational choice without financial penalty, by enabling parents to select the educational environment for their children, gives them rights equivalent to their responsibilities. They should settle for nothing less.

The Ethical Symptom, In a Nutshell

- Simply because most parents, most of the time, deeply want their child's welfare, the family is the natural locus for child nurturing, including introduction to the ethical life of valuing and choosing.
- Such ethical nurturing will reflect the family's specific values, not generic ones.
- The natural way to see the school is as an extension of or aid to family interests and responsibilities.
- In modern democratic societies ethical and cultural pluralism are the forecastable results of social and political freedom.
- In that context, common schools will tend to be ethically inadequate because they will offer either generic and vacuous ethical forms or imposed ones.
- Educational choice without financial penalty can avoid both errors, extend family influence, and sustain a rational ground for ethical pedagogy and behavioral norms.

4

A Primary Cause:
Educational Finance Monopoly

The symptomatic elements of the indictment against American K-12 monopoly schooling are well known, and often treated. As remarked in the introduction, there is perhaps no American industry more flourishing than the industry of "Educational Reform."

The problem with much of that activity, however, is that it is dealing precisely with symptoms of distress, rather than causes. Reduction in class size, mentoring, school-to-work, "values clarification"—these are but a sampling of the "King for a Day" reforms that are constantly being undertaken, and constantly found wanting. Two things should be noted: while such things are not necessarily bad things in themselves, they are all treating symptoms only; and, to the extent any of them are educationally useful, they can be done under school choice as easily, or more easily, than under change-resistant finance monopoly.

And the common shortcoming of all such reforms is that they leave untouched a profound reality which impacts on and contributes to all the symptoms: educational finance monopoly (EFM). Educational finance monopoly (EFM) is an inelegant but analytically accurate term to describe what I take to be the crowning problem with American education at the end of the twentieth century. Educational finance monopoly is the essential cause of the captivity of America's parents. This educational finance monopoly is a *funding* mechanism. It is not in any sense a pedagogical form. It has nothing to do with the modes of education or the content of curricula or anything strictly "educational." It is a funding mechanism by which all tax dollars for education are allocated, and what we discover is that when the monopolistic status quo is defended by its defenders, about whom we will speak much more later, it is protection of the funding mechanism that is their primary objective and the one thing above all things which must be safeguarded. We will discover that many accommodations can be made by EFM defenders to this suggestion and that, this "reform" and that, but never when the suggestion involves allowing anyone but state agents to assign to state schools any of the tax dollars dedicated to education.

The funding mechanism in question, EFM, simply provides all state dollars dedicated to education to public schools and deprives all such dollars from allocation by others (parents) to independent sector schools, creating an illusion on the one hand and a backbreaking penalty on the other. The illusion that is created is that the public schools are in some sense "free," whereas, of course, they are not "free." They are, by comparison with most private sector alternatives, very expensive, indeed. They are paid for by the taxpayers. And the penalty is that the independent schools, in order to function at respectable levels, have to charge tuitions which enable that functioning, and the tuition becomes a penalty for anyone who chooses an independent school. That person is locked in the financial vise of educational finance monopoly. One jaw of the vise is ever-rising taxes to pay for the public schools, and the other jaw of the vise is necessarily increasing tuition to pay for the independent alternative. Many people, unable to pay both taxes and tuition, and having no choice *re* tax liabilities, are in effect deprived of the choice of independent sector schools. Those schools, cut off from normal income flows from otherwise choosing parents, are squeezed, just as the parents themselves are. And the monopoly-protected public schools, not needing to make themselves choiceworthy, are sheltered from the normal human incentives to excel.

In order to grasp the full significance of EFM we must first of all remind ourselves of the general characteristics of monopoly: monopoly is monopoly is monopoly! What we have learned about it around the world and in our own experiences tells us resoundingly of the human destructiveness that monopoly tends to carry with it. If we look at the unraveling of the communist empire in the last half-dozen years, for example, we discover not only the horrors of monopolistic, totalitarian control of coercive power. Those we knew well, through our knowledge of Nazism and its devastating results; and through our knowledge of communist totalitarianism in the age of terror and since. What most people did not know, though many specialists most assuredly did, was the incredibly destructive impact of monopolistic control on the internal life of the communist societies. What it did in those societies was to introduce and formalize a kind of irrationality.

What we know from our own experience in life is that we are imperfect "knowers" of almost all things and that, therefore, we will perfect our knowledge and our mastery and our ability to function to the extent that we open our knowledge to correction and to dialectical progression from less perfect toward more. And what we have learned about the internal life of the communist systems was that their self-protectiveness choked off normal dialectical perfecting within society, so that what looked like an imposing structure from the outside turned out to be in fact nothing but the coercively maintained, but internally hollow, madness of monopolistic structures applied across society to all facets of Soviet and satellite existence. The constitutive elements of those societies, what we would think of as the subsidiary elements of those societies, the churches, the industries and plants, the families, the social organizations, and so on, were simply not permitted to function in any normal fashion. And, as a result, we now know the Soviet economy, for example, was performing horribly, in large part because it was cut off from the kinds of serious knowledge-perfecting that normal competitive dialectical relationships will permit and encourage.

Of course, we do not need to go to the fallen totalitarian regimes to discover the negative and pernicious results of monopoly. When Detroit, the historic leader of the world in automobile manufacturing, increasingly became not even monopolistic, finally, but oligopolistic—simply a less than complete monopolistic development—we discovered the inferiority of their product and its inability to compete effectively with the substantially superior automobiles and trucks being produced elsewhere in the world. The Detroit giants were saved, only in the knick of time, by a renewed sense of competitiveness as they realized, finally, that they had grown fat and sloppy in their self-protective ways. They, their employees, and the whole nation paid an extremely high price for the lessons they had to learn: monopoly-oligopoly does not encourage high quality, efficiency, and attentiveness to consumer welfare and demands.

The fact of the matter is that the negative workings of monopoly are extremely well known to all of us. We would have to be utopians to imagine that the world of American K-12 education, if that world were permitted to operate, as it has operated, under monopolistic circumstances, would somehow avoid the normal destructiveness of monopolies. At the very least, anyone who recognized that educational finance monopoly was the hallmark of contemporary American education funding would recognize, also, that the burden of proof for the desirability of such a system was on its defenders, not on its critics. Monopoly is sufficiently well known as a humanly hurtful device to make us insist, in any logical arrangement, that anyone who wanted to propose it bore the burden of proof.

EFM's defenders sometimes try a gambit along these lines: "Well, after all, government is monopoly and many of the things that government does are monopolistic and therefore there is nothing incongruous about monopolistic school funding mechanisms." Such a gambit will not work. Only at the very essence of the state's responsibilities do we find anything which, in an *a priori* sense, may be thought of as justified monopoly. The state, after all, exists for purposes of insuring that the social fabric is not rent and destroyed by internal conflict and tension, and that its citizens will not be victimized by marauding states beyond its own borders. The state's ultimate capacity, in these regards, manifests itself in police forces and in military arms. To the extent that we find intermediate methods of conflict resolution we do not need to depend on those ultimate weapons of state authority, but the fact is that if we did not have those ultimate weapons, monopolistic weapons, indeed, we would not have a state at all. We would have competitors for being the state. It is only when society achieves something like monopoly in military and police force that it can be said to have established the ultimate guarantor of social order. So from that point of view there is one facet of political organization that is self-evidently justified as monopolistic, and that is the ultimate enforcement devices of military and police authority within the society in question.

Crucially important, even in government itself, what we have discovered and indeed laud, is that in the most advanced forms of government known to man, that is to say, modern democracies, we have replaced monopolistic holding of power with *competitive* holding of power by the device of political parties and alternating governments, and elections that have as their primary purpose precisely putting restraints on the capacity of any group to hold political power for any indefinite period of time. We have built freedom and nonmonopoly into the very heart of the state itself, thereby limiting the pernicious capacity of those few monopolistic power structures we must retain for society's sake. There is simply no argument to be made for an *a priori* certification of monopoly in any facet of government except the ultimate preservation of the social order. And, therefore, it is obviously *not* acceptable to imagine that educational finance monopoly should be presumed to be in some sense an acceptable mode of operation, because, after all, "there are many monopolies in governmental service."

In all other respects, in all *other* things the states does, it really bears the responsibility of the burden of proof, if it wishes to do any of them monopolistically. But what we in America and others in democracies around the world have discovered in the last several decades, of course, is that the burden of proof is too *heavy* for most such state monopolies; that, in fact, they cannot finally be justified and as a result democracies have begun to dismantle them. Even in the private sector, government-protected monopolies, such as AT&T, are being dismantled. The coming break-up of local utilities' monopolies and the opening up of competition in telecommunication, so that even the regional "Baby Bells" must face competition, are further illustrations of the fact that the argument for monopoly has essentially been lost with the exception of the military and police provision noted above.

The fundamental fact is that we have come to understand that under monopoly, when only one *means* is provided to achieve a good *end*, the means comes to be treated as an end-in-itself. When that happens, there is no effective way to evaluate and test the means, and criticism of it is portrayed as an attack on the end itself. That is an irrational and destructive posture and we have come to realize that increasingly well, and to break away from it as a worthwhile mode of satisfying human needs. In general, by contrast, the argumentative presumption for any social organization must be *against* monopoly because monopoly is closed, it tends to be self-serving, it is nonfruitful and nonrational because it is nondialectical and only, indeed, would a utopian start with the assumption that monopoly was fruitful in education.

The fact is at the same time, however, that we have thus far permitted the argument in education funding in the United States to be stood on its head. We have fallen into the evidence trap of accepting responsibility to justify replacing educational finance monopoly, when, in truth, the question properly understood would be how possibly could it *be* justified. We will see in chapter 8 how we got stuck in our current, unfortunate situation. But we should be able to see right now, on purely analytic grounds, that the only rational way to pursue the argument on school funding in the United States would be to acknowledge and recognize that anything that is rightly described as educational finance monopoly can only be justified if the burden of proof is laid on its defenders. They would have to show the negative results of breaking away from monopoly, and would have to show the negative results of choice, in order to defend EFM. Alternatively, and correctly, we would see, on purely analytic grounds, that educational finance monopoly cannot rationally be presumed to be defensible. In chapter 2 we saw, and we will see more, that it is not experientially defensible, either. But our purposes in this chapter are simply to establish the logical order of things. And, in the logical order of things, educational finance monopoly should be "presumed guilty until proven innocent," on the basis of what we know about monopoly generally.

We can next turn our attention to a more specific examination of how the destructive characteristics of monopoly work themselves out, and manifest themselves, in education under the conditions of educational finance monopoly. One of the points that needs to be made early on is that monopolistic policies once in place create structures to maintain themselves, and that is without question the dominant fact of educational finance monopoly. Educational finance monopoly as I have defined it is essentially a funding mechanism, as noted. But no sooner is it established than it begins to sprout personnel, organizations, and structures whose essential purposes in life are to maintain the monopoly from which they come. And, again, there is nothing surprising about this; there is nothing evil. It is the way things work. Interests tend to protect the spigot from which they drink.

Now how do such structures and policies manifest themselves? First of all, and contrary to what many people believe, one of the most pernicious impacts of EFM is on the monopoly's own schools, the public sector's schools, the so-called "public" schools that are in fact just the governmentally owned, maintained, and operated schools. Private schools are "public" in the sense that they serve public purposes, obviously; but they are not governmentally owned and mandated. How does EFM damage the public sector's schools? It does it by keeping from them the normal incentives and stimuli by which human organizations perfect themselves. We normally confront a variety of stimuli to do our work better, to shuck off that which is not working well, and to replace it with that which is working better. That is what happens in a normal give and take comparative-competitive environment in which one means to a given end can be examined in the context of other means. This is mutually beneficial for all of them as they realize they must perform well and they must, in effect, convince people of their desirability. When we remove all such incentives and stimuli from an operating social organization we may have made life easy for those who inhabit it, but we have not taken the steps that will make it better at what it does—just the reverse!

And so, a crucial distinction that has to be made here is that the impact of EFM on its own schools, on the public state-owned schools, is a deleterious impact when we consider them as educational providers. If we consider those schools as fortresses behind which EFM itself is protected, that is a different question. But if we think of them as educational providers and servants of parents and public, which is what first and foremost they are designed to be, then the fact of the matter is that they suffer badly at the hands of educational finance monopoly because they are not encouraged to do their work in superlative fashion. They are encouraged, as a matter of fact, to preserve themselves, maintain themselves, defend themselves. That self-preservative orientation is not fruitful for educational purposes.

But if there is a destructive impact on the public schools, what about the impact of EFM on the independent schools? In a "North Star" natural condition, the parents would be choosing schools and making their selections on the basis of relative value, merit and compellingness. Independent schools would be chosen precisely insofar as they seemed choiceworthy. What happens under EFM, of course, is that the natural approach to the selection of alternative schools is damaged, even set aside, by the financial penalty that attaches to the selecting of an independent school. So dollar supply to such schools depends not just on their quality, but also on the ability of parents to pay the penalty of high taxes and high tuition for their children's participation in the independent schools. Thus, under educational finance monopoly the independent schools suffer, often unto death, because the natural supply of enrollment and therefore of income is artificially choked off by a financial penalty in the act of choosing the independent school. These are the essential realities, the inescapable realities that flow from the policy known as educational finance monopoly and the structures that it spawns once it is in place.

Let us look at some specific ways EFM's basic monopolistic tendencies impact on the whole of our educational life. For example, educational finance monopoly inevitably leads to budgeting in a vacuum, a kind of financial irrationality. In normal budgeting we know what we want, know what we have available to spend, and know the available alternatives and what they cost. That gives us the chance of rational budgeting. We naturally rebel against having just *one* monopolistic supplier, and we know why: without comparison and competition, there is no way to determine the wisdom of an expenditure for goods and services. Thus, monopoly breeds suspicion among consumers.

And not without reason, for the same monopoly encourages unreal budgeting by those protected by it. "Education" and "children" are *good* words, and educational budgets are often defended simply as having children's interests at heart. Anyone questioning such proposals can expect to hear that "he doesn't care for the kids." The truth is, however, that one need not underappreciate children nor their education to question educational expenditures. One may and should question those expenditures precisely because they are proposed in a vacuum, a framework in which comparison and competition do not exist, and overburdened taxpayers routinely are asked to buy what they cannot evaluate.

The central fact of EFM budgeting is that school budgets emerge from a system lacking normal restraints and competitive pressures. Like the rest of us, school administrations are not known for self-restraint, nor are the unions they represent. "More" is the typical budget request. School boards for the most part are expected to be cheerleaders, not serious challengers or generators of alternatives. As the then-superintendent of public instruction told a gathering of Wisconsin school board members, they are to be advocates for *children*, not taxpayers, not even children *and* taxpayers. If they want to show concern for taxpayers, he said, let them join taxpayers' alliances! (*Milwaukee Sentinel*, January 1, 1993). In many places the boards can set their own levy. In such budgetary processes, one finds no mechanisms for ensuring effective and restrained expenditure nor for assuring taxpayers that their dollars are being well-spent.

That is why educational referenda and bond issues often provoke meatax responses: No! The taxpayers are in no position to generate restrained alternatives, but they *can* say "No." Such actions do not *necessarily* mean too much was being asked for or spent on education. Rather, they *necessarily* mean the citizens lost confidence in the budgeting vacuum created by EFM, a system which too often justifies *more* expenditure by pointing to *poorer* performance.

Educational choice without financial penalty will not *necessarily* reduce tax expenditures for education. That depends on variables which can only be assessed in the actual process of budgeting. But what choice will *necessarily* accomplish is to create a context in which competition and comparison naturally occur. Educational alternatives can be assessed rationally. Schools that perform better for less will naturally be favored. And taxpayer confidence can be restored because argument and restraint will be part of the budgeting process.

Every specific educational choice proposal will have a different net financial effect. Most can realistically promise to pay for themselves, even bring savings, by a combination of two factors: each scholarship-bearing student will cost only a fraction of the amount spent on public school students; and some number of those public school students will migrate to less expensive private alternatives. But the possibility of tax savings is not the essential financial difference between EFM and choice. What is essential and undeniably true is something else: with EFM we are engaging in irrational budgeting in a vacuum, and only a utopian would expect good things to happen. With choice we will have the chance to budget intelligently because we will have what we normally insist on in deciding a course of action: comparison and competition among alternative means to the end.

A second and related inevitable characteristic of EFM is that in the schools created under it, there is driven a kind of wedge between the families it is allegedly serving, on the one hand, and the schools that it is maintaining and protecting, on the other. In that kind of an arrangement, where children are bureaucratically assigned rather than being enrolled where parents choose, there is no "natural moral contract" stemming from an act of choice on the part of the parents. There is no parental control; there is no resulting commitment. When "I choose" is replaced by "he is assigned," we have created a relationship between family and school that is fundamentally a divided and wedged relationship rather than an intimate and natural one. As we saw in chapter 3, that which is the *primary* in such an arrangement, that is, parent-child-school relationships, is made to serve that which is *secondary*, that is, the specific educational provider, in this case American public schools.

This distancing of parents from the very heart of education, as a result of monopolistic self-protectiveness, can be illustrated nicely by consideration of two recent, perfectly representative, cases of the mentality monopoly encourages.

The defenders of educational finance monopoly often assert that, while they very much *want* parents' involvement with the monopoly's schools, such involvement is inadequately *provided.* "Don't blame the schools—blame the parents, and the society they reflect," summarizes this attitude. Of course, these same monopoly-defenders react vigorously, even vehemently, against the ultimate and true method for involving parents—school choice without financial penalty. This reaction, while entirely wrongheaded, is at least clearly predictable. After all, EFM's defense is led by people with a direct material interest in that faulty structure, and they see school choice as threatening their monopolistic control over tax dollars.

But this self-protective spirit does not manifest itself only in reaction against school choice without financial penalty. It also comes to the fore when EFM's vested interests imagine that parents are becoming too assertive as regards the monopoly's public schools. This, perhaps even more obviously than opposition to school choice, casts serious doubt on EFM's refrain about wanting more parental involvement. What seems to be wanted is not parental involvement as such, but parental involvement of the "right" type, that is, submissive and controlled parental involvement which can succor and sustain the monopoly's controls over taxes and children.

Consider this 1994 piece put out by the Michigan Education Association, the major educators' union in that state. Entitled "Michigan—The Far Right's New Frontier," the document in question brings fully to mind the sad reality described above. Looked at from EFM's self-protective perspective, there are indeed "right" and "wrong" kinds of parental interests and involvements in the Michigan monopoly's schools. The "right" kind: commit yourself to us and the schools, and leave to us, EFM's vested interests, the overall nurturing of your children. The "wrong" kind of parental involvement is anything which suggests that parents might actually want to evaluate and pass judgment on the quality of the school experience. Such a presumptuous parental attitude would treat the schools as a means to an end, rather than as the ends-in-themselves EFM wants them to be.

To illustrate, a few references from "Michigan—The Far Right's New Frontier," under its first subheading: "WARNINGS." Please note these sample "signals that warn of a Far Right presence" in a locality, each quoted in its entirety:

"Unexpected classroom visits by parents."	(We've got trouble!)
"Increased attendance by same/similar groups of parents at local school board meetings."	(Right here in River City!)
"Demands for copies of documents/records under Freedom of Information Act."	(Parents—that starts with P!)
"Unreasonable demands from parents to be involved in curriculum decisions."	(And that rhymes with T!)
"Complaints about school employees, textbooks/library book selections, or curriculum voiced on local talk shows or expressed in letters to the editor."	(And that stands for trouble!)

My apologies to "The Music Man" for the parenthetic additions. In that splendid musical Professor Harold Hill flimflams the townsfolk of River City by convincing them that a *pool* table (unlike traditional *billiards*) spelt the end of civility and tranquillity in their community, and that only a "Boys' Band" (with uniforms and instruments supplied by him) would restore decency. To brand parents' dedication to and involvement with the educational nurturing of their children as "Warnings," and signals of a "Far Right presence" (itself an undefined smoke screen used as a smear and tar brush) is to display unmistakably the arrogance and self-protectiveness characteristic of monopolies. Let us hope that Michigan's citizens, unlike River City's, are immune to such manipulations. Let us hope that ultimately they insist on having school choice without financial penalty, thus ensuring parents' rights and ending once and for all EFM's stranglehold.

The same monopolistic frame of reference can lead to unmistakably monolithic thinking, also, as the following case makes clear. On October 1, 1993, Wisconsin's assistant superintendent of public instruction spoke some words which are rarely heard from defenders of educational finance monopoly , though they seem implicit in much of what is said by such people. On the Wisconsin Public Broadcast program "Weekend," he said in effect that he seriously doubts whether parents, even those financially able to do so, should be able to send their children to schools of their choosing. This was an unusually bald expression of the monolithic mentality of much of the bureaucratic establishment that has grown up around monopoly-protected public schools.

Before going further, let us set the situation in which this Department of Public Instruction (DPI) representative found himself, and then let him speak for himself. "Weekend" was discussing a Landmark Legal Foundation lawsuit, announced the day before, that aimed to show that the state-supported, limited choice experiment in Milwaukee was unconstitutional because it prohibited parents from choosing sectarian schools, thereby severely limiting their ability to choose among alternatives and violating their religious freedom rights. According to the suit, the Milwaukee program should have been broadened to enable parents to choose religiously oriented schools if they wanted that for their child.

In reacting against the lawsuit, the DPI representative asserted that the suit's objectives violated church-state prohibitions, but this contention was easily refuted by Landmark's Gerald Hill: aid to parents is not aid to churches. Rather than simply acknowledging the refutation, the DPI operative shifted his ground by saying that, even if there were no church-state problem, the Milwaukee program should not be broadened because it would be bad social policy. Correct social policy would presume the superiority of monopoly's public schools for children generally, and the inferiority of any parental judgment to the contrary was the evident implication.

The interviewer saw the radical monopolistic implications of this and the following exchange occurred:

> *The interviewer, incredulously:* "Let me see if I can understand this. You wouldn't argue that there is something wrong with parents sending their children, if they have the money, to private schools, religious schools? That's not wrong? That's not a bad thing?"

> *The DPI Assistant Superintendent:* "Well, I might argue that [it is wrong indeed], because I believe that the need for all folks to go through a common school experience at some time in their life is extraordinarily important for this nation. We are not paying the kind of attention to our pluralism, the kind of commitment to diversity that we need to make."

It may be, of course, that the DPI representative suffered what amounts to a slip of the tongue, that he really did not mean what he said. But he offered no correction. Absent such a self-correction, we are left with his comment and what appears to be its plain meaning, which I would state as follows: "If I, a representative of the monopolistic public education bureaucracy, had my way, there would be little or no private schooling alternative, no practical way for parents rich or poor, black, brown, or white, religious or not, to choose educational options out of concern for their children. For all children should be made to go through the monopoly school experience which I defend as representing 'pluralism' but which, in fact, tramples on pluralism by forcing natural variety into a monolithic one-size-fits-all mold."

To put the best possible interpretation on things, let us assume that our DPI bureaucrat was trying to make a point about the socialization process that is supposed to occur advantageously in the so-called common school. But that is a myth. Private schools produce citizens as dedicated to the common welfare as anyone, and typically more self-disciplined than their public school counterparts. Private schools in major cities are typically more integrated than the public schools, increasingly abandoned by white parents. No, pluralism and diversity, the common good, and educational quality are clearly best served by empowering parents to choose the educational environment their children will experience. In the act of choosing, parents commit to support the school. In making itself choiceworthy, the school, public or private, is encouraged to excel. Thus does choice serve to perfect educational outcomes. The DPI's monolithic vision, by contrast, serves well only the vested interests of educational finance monopoly.

We know that a monopolistic system tends to serve itself and that is not surprising. Nor does it mean that the people who are engaged in so doing are evil. It is, in fact a natural protective instinct, but it is not an acceptable foundation for public policy.

The very core of the problem faced by the parents and citizens of the fifty states is that a means, a funding mechanism meant to *serve*, has, under EFM, become an end-in-itself, as monopolies are prone to do. Such was the powerful message of Dr. Howard Fuller, highly acclaimed Milwaukee Public Schools Superintendent, when he criticized the status quo by saying, as part of his rationale for resigning, that "In this city and other cities around the country, we don't put children first; we put systems first." (*Journal Sentinel*, May 14, 1995) Dr. Fuller, wholly dedicated to Milwaukee's young people, was a classic victim of EFM. But more tragically, so were those very youngsters he can no longer serve.

Part II

A Powerful Cure, Its Worldwide Popularity, How It Might Look in the United States

5

A Powerful Cure:
Parental Freedom via School Choice

In the previous chapter we distinguished between the symptoms and the causes of America's current educational distress. We identified educational finance monopoly (EFM) as a primary cause of many of the problems we are experiencing. School choice without financial penalty attacks and dismantles that primary cause.

School choice without financial penalty can be defined very easily. It simply refers to some or all of tax dollars that have been dedicated to education being allocated or assigned by parents and guardians rather than state bureaucratic educational mechanisms. School choice without financial penalty, in other words, is an alternative *funding* mechanism. As was pointed out in the introduction, in its purest form school choice could be achieved by a policy no more complicated than this: deciding how much money society will spend on providing education, aiming at whatever standards society determines, with agreed-upon quality assurances, such as voluntary accreditation; counting the number of children to be educated; dividing total dollars by number of children and placing the resultant sum, along with any special education or low-income supplements, in the hands of parents and guardians; and then saying to those parents and guardians: "As the persons most dedicated to the welfare of the children, please use the monies here provided to secure for them the very best education you can find, in the kind of educational environment most compelling to you and most harmonious with your family's values."

Any pedagogical forms can be pursued under the rubric of school choice without financial penalty. Indeed, serious educational innovation and experimentation are more easily done under choice than under EFM simply because there is less resistance from the funding status quo. The powerful truth of school choice is that, by permitting no school provider or type to control society's educational dollars, it prevents any means from being treated as an end-in-itself, and thereby provides incentives for all providers to excel. That is what I mean when I say there is no downside risk with school choice, seen from an educational perspective, and compared to the American status quo.

Just as we saw automatic negatives and destructive potentials flowing necessarily from educational finance monopoly, so we will discover, and not be surprised to discover, automatic benefits flowing from school choice without financial penalty. That is, we must here, as in the previous examination of EFM, see and acknowledge the crucial sense in which we can know before the fact many of the good things that will flow from school choice. We will know, also, to avoid the slippery traps of being asked and expected to prove in some statistical sense things that can never be established in that way, things for which true comparisons cannot be drawn. We will not be taken away from the fundamental intellectual task of understanding the internal and inevitable dynamics of alternate systems.

In many respects I think the most fundamental result of school choice without financial penalty, the most defining and determining of its potentials, is what I refer to as the "natural moral contracts of school choice." And here I invite readers to join with me in thinking about the inevitable relationships that occur when voluntary associations have been created, as contrasted with imposed and authority-based associations. In the moral contracts of school choice we discover the simple and undeniable fact that, when parents, students, schools, teachers and staff are freely joined in a free alliance, united around the purpose of educational achievement for the youngsters, we have in that relationship created a series of moral presumptions. It is entirely natural for the parties in that alliance to be beholden one to the other. Again, we know the importance of this in our daily lives. We tend to honor what we have created. We tend to rebel against or treat cynically that which is imposed on us. If we think about this in the context of schools, we will discover what I mean in referring to the moral contracts of school choice.

Take an illustration from my own and others' experience. When the nuns would call our house concerning the behavior of one or another of our children, the message was simple as was the response. The message would go along these lines, "Your son has done [some outrageous thing, let us say thrown a spitball] and we wish you to understand that that is not to occur again." And the response from yours truly would be typically, "Yes, sister. Thank you, sister. We will see to it, sister," and it would not occur again. The reason there was that kind of simplicity and definitiveness in responding was not because of any native meekness, but because of the moral contract that preceded any such incident. We had chosen to be where we were. It was impossible to deny that we were there freely. It was impossible, therefore, to deny the responsibility that existed for us as parents and for the children as students, having asked to join with the teachers and staff of the given school. There is nothing mysterious about this, nothing even very complicated. It is simply what inheres in a freely chosen association. That is the essence of the idea of the natural moral contract of school choice.

There are many vital, automatic attributes that flow from school choice and the moral contracts that are created by it. In chapter 3 we described and lamented the ethical void, for both pedagogical and behavioral purposes, that derives from monopolistic, peas-in-a-pod, schools imposed on a greatly varied and pluralistic society.

Now, if we ask about educational choice as cure or prevention for the moral vacuum proposition that I have developed, what do we see? We see that educational choice naturally extends parental influence beyond the home and into the educational environment, state-run as well as private schools. What educational choice means is providing parents the opportunity, without financial penalty, of selecting an educational environment which they judge to be superior for their child's purposes, including his ethical purposes. In this way, educational choice obviously supports parental values and the ethical foundations on which the youngster can stand as he or she begins developing toward adulthood.

Educational choice, even as it acknowledges and makes room for a common core of civic values and teachings, provides for the naturally pluralistic social and ethical forms that evolve in a free, democratic community. It does not insist on an illiberal homogenization. In this, it precludes the ill effects of an artificial commonality that can create an ethical vacuum, invite secular trends to dominate, undermine the family's values, and make important ethical pedagogy and guidance extremely difficult. Instead, educational choice encourages educational frameworks supportive of or truly neutral toward core family-based values. In turn, that makes morally defined behavioral expectations, standards and norms possible in a way that a generic context for educational work simply cannot provide.

These are the reasons that make it clear to me that the choice of educational finance policy—finance monopoly, on the one hand, parental allocation and choice, on the other—impacts directly on the ethical strength and sensitivities that a society can be expected to manifest. The prevailing conditions in the United States, reflecting not ethical inadequacies of personnel, but the very often unintended effects of injurious structures and policies, are in fact contributing to a kind of ethical juvenility, egocentrism, and lack of self-restraint on the part of American youth. Because of the unfolding logic of educational finance monopoly in a modern pluralistic society, those young people are cut off in substantial part from the natural progression of ethical nurturing, teaching, and guidance that can occur when schooling proceeds from, or is at least compatible with, the home and family. Educational choice without financial penalty, by enabling parents to select the educational environment for their children, gives them rights equivalent to their responsibilities, as they deserve.

Another thing that occurs automatically in a system of school choice without financial penalty is that the parental love, care, and dedication to the welfare of the children which is natural in parents is given the chance to work in the vital area of education. And that fact is the basis of the most fundamental argument for school choice. Enemies of school choice sometimes contend that at its heart school choice is all about "markets" and "privatization." In saying this, they are actually confusing ends and means, and elevating technique over substance. They may welcome such confusion because they imagine that "privatization and markets" can be used as devil words, able to frighten parents and other citizens of good will, as in: "'School choice' *equals* 'privatization and markets' *equals* 'exploitation of your children for somebody else's profit.'"

There are, no doubt, school choice advocates who desire that policy because of a *general* disposition toward markets as superior to monopoly. Recognizing today's school funding method as the educational finance monopoly (EFM) it is, and beginning with a general presumption that markets work better than monopoly, they may simply infer that school choice would be better than EFM. For such people, it could be said, school choice would be a derivative of a preceding conviction about the superiority of markets. There are *many* motives which prompt people to support school choice, and a conviction about "market superiority" is one of them.

But it has little or nothing to do with what appears to motivate most advocates of and workers for school choice. In my experience, most school choice advocates, and parents overwhelmingly, are motivated by a strong conviction that parental freedom is prevented by EFM, and that the great virtues of love and justice, which should dominate and drive schooling, are obstructed by EFM. I do not mean that these are the dominant *terms* used in the struggle for school choice. But I do mean they are the dominant *realities* of that struggle.

The logical bedrock of school choice theory is that the love of parents and guardians for their children is a better guide to the educational welfare of those children than will be the attentions of an inevitably self-serving—not evil, not mean-spirited, but financially self-serving—monopolistic school bureaucracy. Most parents, most of the time, want and will actively seek that welfare. This is a minimalist, not a utopian perspective. They will do this out of a natural *love*—that is, a desire to do for the other—for the child. In order for these parents to act on this love and concern, they require feasible educational alternatives, or school choice. If they have no choices, they cannot act on their concern. Seen from this most basic perspective, interest in a range of options, or a "market," then, is a *derivative* of the prior love and concern.

As to *justice*—the virtue of right proportions, of ensuring for people what is due them—I mean simply this: society fully expects, even demands, that parents accept and discharge responsibility for the nurturing of the child's welfare. So committed are we to the principle of parental responsibility that some jurisdictions are now holding parents legally responsible for vandalistic actions of their children. Parents' duties for the child's welfare is seen to extend to the child's physical, emotional, intellectual, and moral well-being. But under EFM, society turns around and, in effect, says: "Of course we hold our parents responsible for the child's welfare, including educational and moral welfare. But we will *not* empower you accordingly. Indeed, we will impede your efforts, because we will put you in a financial vise—rising school taxes, on one side, and rising independent school tuitions, on the other—which will make it impossible for most of you to choose your child's educational environment." *That* is injustice, a breaking of true proportion between what society expects and what it enables. In the political theory of political rights, there is an old logical rule: that which we *must* do, we *can* do. While that rule seems obvious enough, we must realize that in breaking a true relationship between what we expect of parents and what we enable them to do educationally, we are violating logic and justice.

Thus, a wounded sense of justice, and frustration over the barriers to love's natural course, are the basic motives for most seekers after school choice. Those same motives will work against any undue exploitation by "profiteers." For most school choice advocates, "markets and privatization," though necessary if choice is to be real, are not the end sought but are simply derivative corollaries of the love and justice which precede them. An educational "market," meaning an array of school providers—including state-provided, private including religious, and for-profit if they can make themselves attractive—is just the precondition for the effective living out of love and the effective realization of justice.

Under school choice without financial penalty, all schools, that is to say state and private, will want to be choiceworthy because they must be choiceworthy in order to survive and prosper. What a superior context for improving and perfecting all of education! This is what I mean when I say that all parties involved in the educational equation, parents, children, and schools, and especially public schools, will be the educational beneficiaries of school choice. The financial empowerment of parents, enabling them to select their child's educational environment, has a revolutionary potential to change the whole way contentious issues are looked at and solved. One of today's most vexed issues, for example, is violence in the public schools, especially the schools in major cities. Most monopoly-dictated "solutions" start out by reaffirming the monopolistic status quo, for example, "Now given the public school monopoly system, how do we fix the problem of violence, assault, even killing in our schools?" The answers range from metal detectors to increased security forces, to takeover by municipal police forces.

What happens if, by contrast, we ask an altogether different question? For example, "Would parents choose an unsafe educational environment if they had the choice?" No. "Do some schools, even in the most precarious urban environments, operate with essentially no violence and disruption problems?" Yes. Countless poor, private, effective inner city schools, constructed on the basis of the "natural moral contracts" that come from school choice, provide such environments. They provide them by expecting and demanding them. "Might *all* schools, public and private, find better ways to achieve discipline, decent study environments, and reduced or eliminated levels of violence and disruption if they had to make themselves attractive to parents in order to achieve adequate enrollment?" Yes, that is a reasonable hypothesis. As we will see in chapter 8, questions such as these show the power of the logic of choice to change the basic ways we approach key questions, to overcome the weight of habit and inertia. Choice means letting the love of parents for their children *work*, and it can work even in matters of safety and security.

Choice without financial penalty, then, would make possible and easier the repair of the whole of the educational system. It is a systemic approach. It is not another school reform within the system, the status quo, the educational finance monopoly. It is not one of the "King for a Day" reforms that are so much with us: "Let us get choice in line with the other twelve or fifteen or twenty major educational reforms, and when its time comes, we'll take a look at it." That is an entirely misunderstanding vision of where school choice without financial penalty fits within the framework of educational reform. Educational choice without financial penalty is precisely an attack on the cause, not an attack on the symptoms. But as an attack on the cause, it will in fact impact on all the symptoms that we presently associate with America's educational distress.

It has sometimes been asserted that "choice is not a panacea." In one obvious sense, it is most assuredly not a panacea. There are no panaceas, as a matter of fact. There are things that the simple invocation of school choice will not immediately and automatically fix, such as the serious economic unevenness among students as a reflection of the economic unevenness among parents. It will not fix deprivation in and of itself. But it is as close as we can get to a panacea. It will ramify in all directions. It will, by attacking the cause, directly attack numerous symptoms of educational distress.

The one thing school choice is not is an attack on public schools. It is, instead, a main hope for them. As I suggested above, it is a device which, by introducing those public schools to a new environment of comparison and relative evaluation of performance, can encourage them to perfect themselves, to make themselves more and more choiceworthy. From that point of view, considered as educational providers, the public schools of this nation would in fact be prime beneficiaries of school choice. Nor is school choice without financial penalty an attack on public school personnel. Quite the reverse. Those people suffer no native deficiencies as compared to anyone else, obviously. In many respects they are probably superior people, with altruistic and human-serving orientations. The fact of the matter is, however, that they are also captives of and participants in a series of social and financial structures that are not humanly productive. Those structures are humanly destructive as we saw in the previous chapter. Educational finance monopoly creates structures that defend it and that, in defending it, tend to substitute means for ends and to create fundamental unbalances among things. Educational finance monopoly, as any policy deeply rooted in society, tends to maintain itself, wants to defend itself. Structures grow up for that purpose. Structures are populated by personnel and the personnel are the personnel of the public school monopoly structure. It does not make them bad, but it makes them servants of and advocates for a humanly underperforming enterprise.

It may well be that for those personnel, school choice, if given a chance, would be a boon rather than a bane. If one asks about the recognition of professional status, for example, that at one time did accompany teaching and could once again, that restoration of professional status is far more likely to be achieved under conditions of school choice, one imagines, than under conditions of educational finance monopoly, uniform unionization, and the lack of personnel professionalism in that kind of an environment. One wonders, for example, whether the collapse of the Hartford, Connecticut, school system and its replacement by an entirely contracted educational system, can be attractive to school personnel imagining themselves to be professionals. It seems unlikely.

But we simply cannot accept the utopian presumption that people in a system such as EFM will overcome its natural dynamics, will transcend it. Certainly individuals can. There are such celebrated cases as John Taylor Gatto and David Kirkpatrick and Tom Tancredo who came out of the public monopoly structure, freed themselves from it, became serious critics of it, and, finally, leaders of school choice efforts. But for the most part that is not what one expects. One does not rightly build a system on utopian expectations, and therefore one cannot imagine that EFM in place will begin to reform itself in any basic sense, voluntarily give up monopolistic financial control, or miraculously find a way to keep monopoly while destroying all its symptoms. That is not what happens in life.

Finally, to eliminate the symptoms means eliminating the cause. School choice is a direct attack on educational finance monopoly itself and all the classic monopoly structures and practices which flow from it. School choice without financial penalty would restore the natural order between what we expect of parents on the one hand, and what we enable them to do on the other. It would put in the prime position within the educational structure the fact and dynamic of parental and guardian love and concern. We are presently engaged in a perverse order of educational activity and assignment of resources. School choice without financial penalty would, in and of itself, be a step in the direction of the restoration of natural order. Chapter 6 to follow will show how easily and how well nature can take her course when parents' freedom is assured.

6

A World of Experience with School Choice

As argued above, probably the most fundamental fact of American K-12 education, in place in fifty states and shaping educational outcomes in each of them, is the method by which tax dollars for education are assigned. Those dollars are assigned in each state by governmental bureaucratic structures, and assigned *only* to governmental schools. That is educational finance monopoly (EFM). From it flow many destructive realities, harmful to the governmental schools (operating behind monopolistic structures and deprived of normal incentives to excel); to the independent schools (cut off from support of parents unable to choose them without severe financial penalty); and to parents and children in every state.

The obvious alternative to EFM is school choice without financial penalty. Such a funding approach immediately and automatically would begin to cure many of the problems caused by EFM. But there is a paralyzing tendency among Americans, even many very critical of American education, in effect to proclaim "the educational status quo is loaded with severe problems—but we dare not disturb the status quo!" That people whose material welfare is served by today's educational finance monopoly would talk this way will not surprise us. But why do so many others, such "altruistic corollaries" as PTAs, school boards, newspaper editorial staffs, et al., echo this same self-defeating refrain? Such people, no doubt, are victims of EFM smoke screens (about which chapter 10 will have much more to say) and, in this case, a primary smoke screen is the one that says "No matter how bad things may seem, there are no *known* alternatives, so we had better not trade in the devil we know for ones we know not. The basic 'reforms' people talk about, such as school choice as an alternative to EFM—all these are experimental, untried, hence radical and utopian."

Such an attitude reinforces social inertia and ends up protecting and preserving the EFM status quo, no matter how destructive it may be seen to be. That attitude leads to perpetual new "reforms"—as long as they are confined *within* the system of monopolistic financing, and as long as they protect jobs, benefits, and bureaucratic structures. Such "King for a Day" reforms, by definition, do not reform anything fundamentally, for the *fundament* of today's K-12 reality in America is the funding mechanism itself.

What is even worse is that the premise underlying this dedication to the funding status quo is entirely a myth, an unreal portrayal of the truth of things. That, of course, is the mark of this smoke screen's success. It has led countless truth-loving and truth-telling citizens to imagine that they are, unhappily but truly, trapped in the status quo because of the fearsome unknowability of fundamental alternatives. What is that fact which, if the smoke is cleared, will replace the myth, and free America's citizens and parents to end EFM and replace it with parental freedom? The fact is this: the world is full to overflowing with evidence—experiential, hard evidence—that parental freedom and school choice work splendidly, just as logic would suggest they would. As often noted, much of that evidence is close at hand, for example, the unqualified success of the G.I. Bill after World War II, Korea, and so on; the positive results of state-based tuition grants in helping to preserve an independent option among colleges; the effectiveness of preschool voucher programs in many states, usable at independent institutions, including religious ones. All these facts are success stories, and all are comparable to and encouraging of extending school choice to K-12 education in America.

Still at home, and in many respects the most useful experience of all, is the story of America's Catholic schools. In the nineteenth century and through much of the twentieth, they provided true "school choice" to America's Catholic families. True school choice means not just the freedom to choose non-state schools, but the freedom to do so *without financial penalty*. And the pastors, parishes, and religious sisters gave exactly that capacity to Catholics, as they and the Church sought what all parents instinctively want: a school environment compatible with and supportive of the family's values. Who can deny that the schools thus created were, and are, on balance excellent places for education, as are the other, comparable schools created by other religious communities for similar reasons?

Thus, it is truly the case that school choice on our own shores and in our history has long since proven itself, in such analogous experiences as those summarized above. As powerful a myth-dispelling fact as that is, however, it pales by comparison with the overwhelming evidence in favor of school choice provided by the national stories told ever so briefly in this chapter. These lessons from abroad summarize the outstanding effects of parental freedom to choose schools without financial penalty in just four democracies, though true choice in some form is characteristic of democracies worldwide—but not for the U.S.! The four cases here described represent different specific approaches to a common end: the empowerment of parents, so that their *rights* can be comparable to their *responsibilities*. Such symmetry between what society expects and what it makes possible is, obviously, exactly what comes logically and naturally, once one thinks about it.

The four democracies used here are directly comparable not to the much larger United States as a whole but to many specific American states. And it is in the states, of course, that America does its schooling. Thus, we see the direct comparability and utility of these foreign cases. Despite this pertinence, American insularity, and the successful smoke screens of EFM's defenders, have been remarkably effective in preventing others' experiences from shedding light on our own situation. The insularity reminds one of the famous British headline of the 1930s: "Fog Continues— Continent Cut Off!" Fog and smoke continue, indeed, and they continue to victimize unsuspecting Americans. Lacking American-style constitutional complications *re* church and state, other democracies typically fund independent schools directly, rather than using indirect devices such as tuition vouchers. But that is an entirely inconsequential distinction, since, as our cases will show, their independent schools operate with full freedom and are entirely parent-driven, just as will be all American schools in the age of school choice without financial penalty.

As the first step in blowing away this "no experience" smoke screen, we will look briefly at the actual school choice programs in four modern democracies. These vignettes were first put forth in the Blum Center's *Educational Freedom Report* #10, June, 1994, having been prompted by the publication that spring of *School: A Matter of Choice* by the Center for Educational Research and Innovation of the Organization for Economic Co-operation and Development (OECD). All the citations in the four national summaries to follow are from that volume, and the summaries themselves were largely the work of Mr. Nicholas A. Freres, then a Blum Center Associate. After seeing these snapshots, we will draw from them some of the many lessons they can provide Americans, and provide brief documentary displays which show the greatly natural and productive educational results which come from putting parents' rights at the foundation of a nation's educational policy.

Four Case Studies: Parents Empowered to Choose

Australia

In 1973, Australia, under the leadership of a liberal-leaning Labour government, adopted choice in education by establishing a system of financial support for the nation's private schools. As a result, many Australian families who could not otherwise have afforded to do so have been able to choose private schooling for their children. An indication of that is the growth in private school enrollments under Australia's school choice system: from 21 percent of total enrollments in 1971 to 28 percent in 1992 (p. 55). The majority of private schools in Australia are religiously affiliated. Interestingly, although Australia's constitution prohibits the establishment of religion by the state, in language strikingly similar to the U.S. Constitution's First Amendment, Australian courts have determined that government support for children's education in religious schools does not violate that prohibition (pp. 43, 57).

Australia provides support for private schools and private schooling systems—such as the nation's system of Catholic schools—both at the Commonwealth (i.e., the federal) level and at the state levels of government. The amount of aid depends upon the wealth and resources of the private school, with the neediest schools receiving a larger share of the aid. Private schools are categorized according to their wealth and located in one of twelve "bands." Higher bands represent needier schools and lower bands represent wealthier schools. The amount of aid provided by the Commonwealth varies from 12 percent to 49 percent of the average per-pupil cost in the public schools; while the amount contributed by the states varies from 20 percent to 25 percent of the average public school per-pupil cost (p. 55). "Thus a poor school in a high 'band' whose costs are lower than the public average can come close to total government funding, while a private school charging a high fee and spending more than the average per pupil recoups only a small proportion from government" (p. 56). For the benefit of children from low-income families, many private schools in Australia waive the portion of their fees not covered by government aid—a practice that is particularly prevalent among the nation's Catholic schools, which are noted for enrolling students from all social backgrounds.

The educational choice policy established in 1973 provides aid for recurrent or per-pupil costs. In 1986, however, Australia went a step further and adopted a policy known as the New Schools Policy, "under which new non-government schools will be supported, in terms of capital as well as recurrent funding. Committees in each state and territory make recommendations attempting to reconcile planning and efficiency with choice and diversity" (p. 56). Moreover, some states in Australia (the OECD report mentions New South Wales and Victoria) have implemented policies allowing public schools to become specialized schools or to become self-managing. As a consequence, these public schools have not only made themselves more attractive to parents and students, but they have also developed reputations for expertise in their specialty fields. Cherrybrook Technology High School in New South Wales is a case in point: it has become so successful in its specialty field—modern technology—that it now serves as a center of instruction for other teachers (p. 116-17). Having opened the door to genuine choice in education in 1973, Australia has begun to introduce and permit innovation throughout its education system.

Two public schools in Melbourne may also serve to illustrate the dynamic educational atmosphere created by choice. Mount Waverly Secondary College is known for its rigorous academic instruction and is located in a wealthy suburb (p. 111). Doveton Secondary College, on the other hand, has developed a reputation as "the district's science and technology centre" (p. 113). Doveton is located in a poorer Melbourne neighborhood. Despite their differences in orientation and location, both schools have proved successful in attracting students and feel confident of their ability to compete with private schools. Perhaps most revealingly, both schools maintain inviting policies regarding inspections and visits by parents, and both promote their programs at local primary schools. Of course, private schools—and the families that choose them—have also benefited from Australia's education policies. Maranatha Christian School, located in the same poorer neighborhood of Melbourne as Doveton Secondary College, "distinguishes itself by a stress on high standards of behaviour and Christian teaching" (p. 113). Under choice, its enrollments have grown from ninety-seven students in 1971, when it began operation, to 750 in 1993. The OECD report also notes the sustained success of two Catholic secondary schools for girls in

Melbourne. Avila College, located in the wealthier suburb, has an enrollment of 950 (p. 112); while Killester College, in the same poorer neighborhood as Maranatha and Doveton, enrolls 788 girls (pp. 113–114). In order to make themselves attractive to parents, both schools rely on their reputations for providing religious "pastoral care" for their students. Neither school refuses admission to girls from families who cannot afford to pay the modest tuition fees.

Denmark

Families in Denmark have long enjoyed their country's well-established educational choice program. The forthright support accorded educational choice in Denmark is echoed by the Danish Ministry of Education: "An important feature of the Danish educational system's democratic structure is the access to a school of your own choice. If the schools offered by the public education system are not to your liking, you can attend a private school, of which there are 408 spread throughout the country." ("The Folkeskole," Danish Ministry of Education and Research) In order to make such access to private schools a reality, the Danish government provides financial aid equivalent to approximately 72 percent of the average public school per-pupil cost for each student enrolled in a private school (p. 145). This policy allows Danish private schools to charge exceptionally low tuition fees. For this reason, private schools in Denmark are known as "free schools."

Smaller free schools have always received a larger proportion of aid. This policy helps to compensate for the smaller schools' higher than average costs and it means that free schools can afford to open and sustain themselves in smaller towns and rural areas. Thus, also, are families throughout the country assured of access to free schools. When it became apparent in 1991 that adjustments in the aid proportions were needed, the funding system was easily altered by the Danish government to the satisfaction of all (pp. 145, 146). Under the altered funding system, the government establishes the general level of aid and allows the free schools association to determine precise proportions for distribution. Today, smaller free schools still receive a larger proportion of aid, while free schools with larger enrollments receive what they need to maintain their low fees.

Parental commitment to and involvement with free schools is viewed as an integral component of their success. The Danish policy requires that free schools charge some tuition fees, albeit very low fees, in order to ensure that parents have a financial stake in—and thus a high degree of commitment to—the school they choose for their children (p. 145). Additionally, as a means of assuring direct parental control of free schools, each one "must be governed by a board elected by parents" (p. 145).

The most significant feature of parental control under any educational choice program, however, is the option to withdraw children from a poorly performing school and send them to a preferred one. This parental capacity, in turn, directly encourages the schools to perform up to parents' expectations. The experience of the Albertslund Lilleskole (or 'little school') illustrates the point nicely (p. 147). The Albertslund was founded as a free school near Copenhagen. Designed to appeal to parents with left-leaning political beliefs, the school offered a liberal pedagogy with little in the way of traditional curriculum and classroom discipline. As parents became increasingly concerned about student performance at the school, however, enrollments began to decline. Eventually, Albertslund reformed its curriculum, offering more instruction in basic academic subjects. The school also replaced the original policy of parental involvement through service on various school committees with a new policy of encouraging direct parental participation in the class-rooms. The result: Albertslund Lilleskole's "rolls rose from 60 to 150" (p. 147).

Denmark's respect for parental choice has resulted in free schools that are genuinely free of any government interference (p. 145). It has also led to a flourishing of a great variety of free schools. "They include independent rural schools, academically-oriented lower secondary schools, some religious schools, progressive free schools, Rudolf Steiner [i.e., Waldorf] schools, German minority schools and immigrant schools such as Muslim schools" (p. 146). For example, as Danish society has developed a more pluralistic character, its parental choice of schools has led naturally to growth in the independent sector, which now enrolls more than 10 percent of Danish students. The Danish educational choice program has also brought improvements to the public schooling system, known as the "folkeskole" or system of folk schools. Public "schools are starting to replicate the model of parental involvement developed in free schools. In 1989, school boards with a majority of parent members were established at all folk schools, and increasing decentralisation to these boards is foreseen. Parents are also gradually obtaining a freer choice of folk school within their municipality" (p. 147).

The Netherlands

Comprehensive choice in education was established as the central education policy of the Netherlands in 1917. It has remained so to this day. Private schools in the Netherlands are available to all regardless of income because public and private schools are financed "on a completely equal basis" (p. 67). The extent to which the Dutch avail themselves of the educational opportunities offered by this policy is reflected in the high proportion of private school enrollments: more than two-thirds of all Dutch students attend private schools (p. 68). School choice in the Netherlands enjoys strong political and popular support, as one would expect, and it has, quite naturally, yielded a rich diversity of educational alternatives reflecting the nation's religious and cultural pluralism. Educational choice in the Netherlands is not limited to the private sector, however: "The Dutch belief in the right to choose schools is reflected also in liberal rules for choice within the public sector" (p. 69). Ordinarily, parents are able to choose from among any of the public schools located in their municipality, although some larger cities confine public school choice to smaller, submunicipal districts.

To qualify for funding, private schools must maintain minimum levels of enrollment established by the Dutch government (pp. 23, 31, 68). In practice, this means that existing private schools must strive to remain sufficiently attractive to parents to sustain their required minimum enrollment, at the risk of losing their funding. It means, also, that educators seeking to found a new school must demonstrate that the school would fulfill a genuine demand on the part of parents. Minimum enrollment levels, quite sensibly, vary greatly from municipality to municipality, depending on the size of the local school-age population. Moreover, enrollment requirements are eased when school closures would threaten educational diversity in a given locality. This policy not only illustrates the Dutch commitment to assuring access to a variety of schools, it also serves the very practical goal of making "the choice of more than one school a reality in many small communities" (p. 31).

The OECD report observes that in response to parental preferences and choices, Dutch schools tend in the direction of "educational conservatism" with a focus on "fundamental values" (p. 36). This, of course, is not surprising, since, as the report points out, parents are generally reluctant to submit their children to educational experimentation. One can easily imagine the dire fate of educational fads in a country with genuine parental choice such as the Netherlands. But the OECD report also notes that in the Netherlands schools offering solid alternative pedagogical approaches—such as Montessori and Waldorf—"are growing rapidly" (p. 29).

Perhaps the most striking feature about education in the Netherlands is the prevalence of religious schools. In 1990, a remarkable 63 percent of all primary school students and 64 percent of all secondary school students attended religiously affiliated schools representing a wide range of denominations (p. 68). The tremendous popularity of religious schools cannot be attributed to perceptions of academic superiority. For in the Netherlands under genuine choice in education, unlike conditions in the United States, the public schools are not commonly believed to offer inferior academic instruction, even in larger urban areas (p. 70). Indeed, in the Dutch city of Haarlem, the most academically prestigious school is a public secondary school (p. 95).

In part, the success of religious schools in the Netherlands can be explained by their willingness to respond and adapt to changing social circumstances (p. 69). For example, many Catholic schools in bigger cities (the OECD report mentions The Hague and Rotterdam) readily admit large numbers of non-Catholic students—a practice that is also common among urban Catholic schools in the United States. But the commitment of religious educators to providing educational opportunities to urban schoolchildren of all faiths cannot alone account for the widespread popularity of religious schools in the Netherlands. The OECD report offers a more telling explanation: "The most frequent reason seems to be choice of their [the religious schools'] ethos, which is sometimes perceived to be more in keeping with a family's values than the secular system" (p. 28). Given a real choice, as in the Netherlands, most parents will choose to send their children to a school that reflects their values. Even among families that do not belong to the denomination represented by a religious school, many nonetheless prefer such a school for their children. Another aspect of a school's ethos is its attitude toward its students, which is often believed to be of a distinctive quality in religious schools. By way of illustration, Catholic schools in the Netherlands, as in Australia, are generally thought "to offer a familial atmosphere in which the character and development of the individual is given attention" (p. 28). A "familial atmosphere" would obviously be an attractive feature of a school for many parents, as well as a significant factor in the academic success of many students.

Sweden

Of the four countries discussed here, Sweden's adoption of full-scale parental choice in education is the most recent and, in some ways, the most dramatic. By the early 1980s, independent alternatives to the public schooling system in Sweden had been all but entirely eclipsed. Private school enrollments at the time accounted for a mere 0.6 percent of the total (p. 82). Swedish parents, however, had grown increasingly dissatisfied with the "monochrome" character of the public schools as well as with an "unresponsive" attitude on the part of school officials (pp. 32, 79, 84). Largely in response to this widespread dissatisfaction, the Swedish government undertook a number of reform measures in the early 1990s designed to increase educational options, both within the public school system and between public and private schools.

Perhaps the most significant of these measures is a 1992 law establishing an education grant program for students attending private schools. The March, 1992, Government Bill on Freedom of Choice and Independent Schools declares, "The right and opportunity to choose a school and education for one's children is important in a free society." It adds, "The goal is to achieve the greatest possible freedom for children and parents to choose their school." Beyond the "vital principle" of freedom of educational choice, the bill describes some of the additional anticipated benefits of choice in education: "a greater sensitivity to the wishes of students and parents on the part of schools"; the growth of "a multiplicity of educational options and pedagogical methods"; the improvement of all schools through the "stimulus" of choice; and the creation of "incentives for cost efficiency." Although the bill and the school choice program it established are only a few years old, the evidence of choice's beneficial effects has begun to build in Sweden.

Under the 1992 law, grants are provided to private schools based on their enrollments. The grants are worth "at least 85 per cent of the cost of educating a pupil in the local municipal system, multiplied by the number of pupils in the school" (p. 80). These education grants have enabled private schools in Sweden to reduce substantially or, what is more frequent, to waive altogether their tuition fees. During the 1992–93 school year, 90 percent of private schools participating in the program charged "no fees at all" (p. 80). As a result, in the program's first year, private school enrollments jumped 20 percent (p. 80). Keeping pace with the newborn demand for independent alternatives, the number of private schools in Sweden has grown rapidly—indeed, the number *doubled* in the first year of choice, according to Swedish officials (p. 80), and has continued to mushroom since. Montessori and Waldorf schools have been quite popular with Swedish parents, and under choice their number is rising. The supply of religious schools, representing a variety of denominations, has increased greatly under Sweden's educational choice grant program. The OECD report notes especially the growing popularity of "schools of an Evangelical Christian character" (p. 83). A third type of private school that has begun to appear in Sweden with increasing frequency is known as an "ordinary" school (p. 83). Ordinary schools are independent community-based schools organized by parents and educators, often in response to decisions by municipal officials to close an existing school or to decline to open an additional public school. Clearly, school choice has prompted many Swedes to take a more active role—and in some cases a decisive role—in the education of their children. And just as clearly, choice has encouraged a multiplicity of educational options and methods to flourish, as the program intended, and shows that, under choice, educational supply is not static but dynamic.

Along with the 1992 program giving Swedes real opportunities to select private schools, policies have been adopted to increase diversity and choices within the public school system. Although rules vary from municipality to municipality, many now allow parents to choose from among local public schools, "with money following pupils" (p. 79). While most Swedes continue to enroll their children in the nearest public school, "the power of choice...has started to change their relationship with that school" (p. 84). Schools have begun to open themselves to inspection by parents, and "[public school] principals in Stockholm say they are putting increasing stress on involvement with parents, knowing that they will be the best advertisers to attract more enrolments in the school" (p. 35). One of those principals observed, "It is of great value for a school to be examined," and another acknowledges that "competition improves the quality" of schools (p. 110).

What Can the Cases Say to Us?

The first and most obvious thing to learn from these four illustrations is that school choice is neither experimental nor untried nor utopian. It is natural and common among modern democracies which take seriously the assumption that parents' rights should match their responsibilities. Coupled with our own vast analogical experiences with forms of school choice, as noted above, the positive histories of other nations with school choice should refute definitively the "experimental" smoke screen.

Another very important reality of school choice is that it is inherently flexible and opens easily to any rational form of educational variety. While under it watchful parents are unlikely to encourage or sustain fanciful experimentation with their children's education, any serious alternative can come forth easily, without the obstructions to change which can be expected and observed in our monopolistic system.

Other important inferences to be drawn from the OECD study, and from the general observation of school choice in other nations include:

- even in particularly homogeneous societies there is a natural supply of educational alternatives that will emerge if financial *penalties* for choosing them are replaced with *incentives*;
- parental involvement in schools, state-owned or private, is a natural corollary of choosing among them, and this illustrates the "moral contract" which accompanies voluntary actions;
- parental esteem for the chosen school, *and* for the ability to choose, is an unsurprising companion;
- in schools chosen rather than imposed it is entirely customary to find relatively disciplined and orderly educational environments;
- the mere fact of comparison and competition which choice brings provides great stimulus to improve all schools, state and independent, as one would expect;
- parental concern for the child's welfare clearly extends to concern for the ethical standards of schools under consideration;
- one manifestation of this is the relative strength of religious schools when financial penalty is removed from choosing them;
- and, while acknowledging the difficulties of measuring educational outcomes and hence statistical "quality," OECD's work shows conclusively that school characteristics normally associated with educational achievement are routinely encouraged by choice.

The plain and powerful truth that school choice without financial penalty works easily, naturally, and productively wherever it has been employed should come as no surprise to us, of course. We know from countless perspectives that free choice is superior to monopoly in human enterprises generally. And we know that the love and concern parents and guardians typically have for the children under their care is a better guide to those children's welfare than is any monopolistic, bureaucratic system of assignment. The surprise would be if such basic realities did *not* apply to education and educational funding.

But if we know all these things (and we do), then from them we know one more: America's parents have up to now been prevented from having the school choice which is their right *not* because of any deficiencies in such choice, nor uncertainties about it. It has been obstructed for purely political reasons—political manipulation to protect financial interests fed by today's monopoly. Probably because no one wants frontally to defend or even to use the word "monopoly"; and no one wants frontally to diminish parents' rights and prerogatives; we hear euphemisms and smell smoke. But over the din and through the haze, and with the help of others' favorable experiences, we can better hear and see the truth: parental freedom and school choice without financial penalty are natural, right, and educationally beneficial to those who experience them. *It is not parents' rights which need justification, but anything which obstructs those rights.*

Selected Documentary Illustrations From the Four Nations

The following brief documents have been selected and are here reproduced for a very particular reason. The essential mechanisms of choice in the four nations have been described summarily above, and need not be repeated here. The statutory provisions in the several nations are too cumbersome and particular to be useful. Instead, what follow are various documents from the four nations which accomplish a common thing: they show in each case how natural, common-sensical, and even obvious is the educational funding policy we call "school choice without financial penalty." When a society begins to develop pluralistic characteristics; and if it takes parents' rights seriously; then, unless artificially obstructed by something like America's EFM, that society's natural political dialogue, precisely in a common-sense way, will lead it to school choice. Readers will see this plain truth displayed simply and often in the ensuing documentary descriptions of policy intention in our four sample nations.

Australia

The following brief passages from the Australian Department of Employment, Education and Training clearly display the basic approach

Australia has taken to achieving educational excellence *via* parental freedom.

Main Aims of School Choice

Rationale for Funding Non-government Schools

Federal Government policy supporting choice over the last twenty years has been developed in the context of funding policy for non-government schools. There have been two basic rationales for the provision of public funds to non-government schools:

- to ensure adequate resource levels in all schools (a 'needs rationale')
- to give all students a basic level of financial support in the school of choice, irrespective of resource level (an 'entitlement rationale').

State and territory governments, with the exception of Victoria, also allocate at least a proportion of their funding to non-government schools as flat rate per capita grants, with the proportion allocated on the basis of need varying between states/ territories (usually between 20–25 per cent of government costs).

The Interim Committee for the Australian Schools Commission (the Karmel Committee, 1973) provided a rationale for funding non-government schools with the following elements:

- Australians were choosing to send their children to non-government schools based in various religious denominational groupings;
- the cost of providing adequate quality of education was beyond the resources of many of these schools;
- government intervention was designed to raise the standard of provision without necessarily funding an expansion in non-government school participation.

The issues of choice and quality were therefore central to the Commonwealth's decision to expand funding to the non-government school sector. (Emphasis added.)

(*School Choice: Background Report for the Centre for Educational Research and Innovation* of OECD, from the Australian Department of Employment, Education and Training, 1993)

Denmark

The following citations from Danish policy statements show the common-sense evolutions which occur if one starts with two vital premises: first, parents' capacity should equal what we expect from them; second, any particular school or system of schools is rightly seen as a means to the end of high educational quality, not as an end in itself.

In Denmark all children between the age of 7 and 16 must receive education but— provided a certain minimum standard is obtained—it is a matter of choice for the parents whether the education is received

1) in the publicly provided municipal school,

2) in a private school, or
3) at home.

Number of schools and pupils
About 10% of all children at basic school level (including the voluntary pre-school and 10th form) attend private schools. In 1991, approx. 70,000 children attended 409 private schools, while 540,000 pupils attended the municipal school of which there are approx. 1,800.

Types of schools
Private schools in Denmark may be roughly divided into the following categories:

* small "Grundtvigian" independent schools in rural districts,
* academically oriented lower secondary schools (the so-called 'réal'-schools),
* religious or congregational schools such as Catholic or Danish Mission schools,
* progressive free schools,
* schools with a particular pedagogical aim, such as the Rudolf Steiner schools,
* German minority schools,
* immigrant schools such as the Muslim schools.

The bottom line is that private schools will be recognized and receive government financing regardless of the ideological, religious, political or ethnic motivation behind their establishment. (Emphasis added.)
Some private schools are very old, some are quite new, and new ones are still being added. It is characteristic of the private schools that they are smaller than the municipal schools.

Legislation
All parties in the Danish Parliament want legislation ensuring financial support for private schools, *partly based on the notion that also the municipal schools will benefit from the experience and competition offered by the private schools.* (Emphasis added.)
The legislation contains detailed rules about government financial support but only the most general rules about the educational content. There are for example almost no rules about the Ministry of Education's control of the educational performance of the schools. However, the schools may always come to the Ministry for advice if and when they need it, and the Ministry can take special action, if needed.

Educational content
All that is demanded of private education is that it measures up to that of the municipal schools. The Ministry of Education confers on private schools the right to use the municipal schools' final examination and thereby exercises a form of indirect quality control. *However, in principle it is not up to any government authority but to the parents of each private school to check that its performance measures up to the demands of the municipal schools.* (Emphasis added.)
It is the parents themselves who must choose a supervisor to check the pupils level of achievement in Danish, arithmetic, mathematics, and English. If the school is found inadequate, the supervisor must report it to the municipal school authority who may then assign the children to other schools. Individual parents who are dissatisfied with a private school may move their child to another private school or to a municipal school. The local municipal school must always admit the child.
In extraordinary circumstances, the Ministry of Education may establish special supervision, for example if there is reason to believe that the school teaches

Danish so poorly that the children's ability to cope with life in Denmark may be impaired.

In recent years, there has been a development towards decentralization within the municipal school (the Folkeskole) system which may be said to be a "free school-model" within the framework of the municipal Folkeskole. Generally speaking, the municipal school has the same curricular structure in all parts of the country, but there is a wide scope of variety based upon local government decisions. The Act on the Folkeskole of 1989 decentralized a great number of decisions to the new school boards where the parents are in the majority. The Act also provided the parents with a free choice of school within their local community.

(*Private Schools in Denmark*, Danish Ministry of Education and Research, 1994)

The Netherlands

In many respects, the Dutch educational funding policy known as "pluri-formity" is a model for all nations, and it is well-described in the following Dutch documents.

While centralisation proved to be an extremely effective method of creating an education system, slowly but surely the calls for greater autonomy became more vociferous. This movement was part of the general social trend dominated by liberalism and largely motivated by the desire for diversity and independence in certain sections of the community and the wish *not* to see power vested solely in the government.

In 1848 the Netherlands, already a kingdom for 35 years, acquired a Constitution which embodied the freedom to provide education. The same liberal thinking on the Constitution meant a withdrawal by central government from school government and management; the state no longer had a monopoly on schools or education. The municipal authorities became more involved in managing and running schools. Publicly-run schools, entirely financed by the government were to be ideologically neutral, but nevertheless based on general Christian principles which meant there was no place for doctrinal teaching within the public schools. Private schools could be set up for this purpose but these were not financed by the government. This state of affairs led to what had become known as the 'schoolstrijd' ('schools' issue') which was a determining feature of Dutch politics for about 70 years, between 1848 and 1917.

Both Protestants and Catholics objected to the neutral principles of publicly-run schools. They demanded either that publicly-run schools should be frankly denominational or that private denominational schools should also be financed by the government. The schools' issue came to an end in 1917 with private primary schools being put on a completely equal financial footing with publicly-run schools. *Freedom to provide education became a social right. Nowadays the financial equality applies across the board.* (Emphasis added.) Extensive use has been made of the opportunity to found private schools with government financial backing. For every 26 state primary and secondary schools there are about 74 private schools, which explains the restricted role that the government still has when it comes to educational issues and policy. The government has of course its responsibility in this regard but it is exercised in conjunction with the various groups in the education field. An outsider might easily form the impression that this was an untenable situation, but despite the great variety of opinions among the Dutch there is also a large measure of agreement on many educational matters. The organisational set-up enables discussion to be focused on matters of common interest. The present state of Dutch education bears testimony to the fact that such pluriformity is a workable proposition. (*Education and Science*, The Kingdom of the Netherlands, 1984)

Simplified Expression of Current Policy
    Anyone in the Netherlands is free to provide education (Article 23 of the Constitution). This means that schools can be set up by private initiative and run by societies or foundations. Schools of this kind are called private schools, as opposed to those that are established and run by government, which are called public-authority schools. Private schools are often founded on the basis of religious or other beliefs. Publicly-run and privately-run schools are funded according to the same criteria. *The competent authority is responsible for what goes on in the schools, in so far as this is subject to statutory provisions.* (Emphasis added.) Central government is the competent authority for state schools, the municipal authorities for local-authority schools and *the school boards for private schools.* (Emphasis added.)

(*The Dutch Education System*, Dutch Ministry of Education and Science, 1988)

Sweden

Sweden's traditionally limited school choice was expanded greatly in the early 1990s, as noted above. The following Swedish materials explain plainly the parent-serving reasons for that change.

A School for Each and Everyone
    It is in the school that the future is being built. The school shall provide children and young persons with fundamental and lasting knowledge. It shall also transmit the norms and values upon which our society rests. It is to a very large extent in school that we are moulded into citizens and become social beings. For this reason the school shall stimulate critical thinking, develop a thirst for knowledge and build on the eagerness and curiosity that exists in all children.
    Results and success are determined largely by the involvement of pupils, teachers and parents in the school. Good working relationships between the school and the home have a vital role to play in shaping the environment in which knowledge and growth take place. The sense of community that develops between pupils is a foundation for life.
    People, however, are not identical. Children just like adults have different personalities, interest and potentialities. For this reason not all schools can be the same.
    Now, however, pupils and parents have the right and the opportunity to choose a school that is right for them. What they choose will depend on a number of factors— the location of the school, how it is run, and whether it has any specific orientation in its teaching.
    It is an important goal that the Swedish school shall cater for everyone. The foundations of development and welfare—for both the individual and society as a whole— are laid only when all children in a society have the opportunity of going to school. A

school for all must also mean a school that can be adjusted to the differing needs, circumstances and interest of the individual.

For freedom of choice to exist, parents and pupils must be able to choose freely between different types of schools. For this reason it must not only be possible to start independent schools, they must also have the right to receive public grants. This will ensure that all pupils have the opportunity of making a choice between municipal and independent schools. (Emphasis added.)

The proposals for the new curriculum and marking system give the individual school the right and responsibility to decide on how important parts of the education shall be formed. In this way every school—municipal as well as independent—can determine both the teaching and pedagogical approach that is most appropriate for them and which corresponds to the desires of parents and children. The right to choose thus becomes both a prerequisite and the impetus for a dynamic, modern school.

The right of parents and their children to choose a municipal or an independent school creates greater involvement which leads to increasing sensitivity to the needs and interests of parents and pupils. A whole range of different types of schools will emerge, each with its own special orientation, personality and competence. The result will not be just standard schools for everyone, but individual schools catering for the interests and abilities of individual pupils.

The right to choose a school is a right that everybody has. It aims at giving pupils and parents a greater influence in schools and as a result leads to the creation of a school that focuses on the individual pupil. The new curricula for compulsory and upper secondary schools mean that every school—both municipal and independent—has the opportunity of developing the most appropriate ways of teaching. As a result teachers, parents and pupils can together help to create better schools.

As the independent schools qualify for public grants, they can be run without charging high fees. The choice of school will thus no longer be a question of private wealth. (Emphasis added.) In future the municipalities when planning their activities will have to take into account the distribution of students between municipal and independent schools. In this situation, grants to independent schools will no longer be regarded as an extra burden on education that could have been provided within the framework of municipal activity. (*The Right to Choose School*, Swedish Ministry of Education and Science, 1994.)

7

It Can Be Done Here, Too:
American School Choice Examples

In chapter 6 we saw how simple and easy it is to put parents in the saddle of their children's education where nature is permitted to take her course. In the United States, massive obstructions block the path of parental freedom and mastery in education. In the following chapters, we will look at why parental prerogative is so badly obstructed, who is primarily responsible for the obstructing, and how they go about that obstructing business. For now, let us simply recognize that American school choice proposals are a very motley collection of efforts rightly reflecting substantial differences among the fifty different political jurisdictions out of which they evolve.

But American school choice efforts up to this point reflect a great deal more than the differentiations among their state jurisdictions. They all reflect as well the torturous need to satisfy the objections and problems of an errant status quo even as they propose to leave it. Thus, choice efforts consistently are confronted by the bad traits of the status quo as reasons for *not* changing from the status quo to school choice. They may be told, for example, as they are routinely told, that any up-front costs associated with the shift to school choice make it impossible to add school choice to the panoply of educational arrangements because "it will break the budget"—already broken by overexpenditure and underperformance. Or they are told that it will result in the flight of good students from the bad system. What an ironic and terrible condemnation of the status quo! "Skimming" is the name usually given to this tremendously interesting, even humorous, reason for not shifting to choice. Or, as recently arose in discussions involving possible school choice efforts in the District of Columbia, we are told without even an acknowledgment of the humor of the situation, that we cannot move to school choice in the District of Columbia because, after all, there is no substantial supply of empty seats available in the independent schools.

The irony of this, of course, is that there is little supply of seats in the independent schools in the District of Columbia because the educational finance monopoly status quo has killed off so many actual and "would have been" independent schools, literally killed them off, by squeezing them to death in the financial vise of rising taxes and rising tuitions. A companion reason for there being so little supply in the District is because the private schools that do remain are filled because of the desperation of District parents over the condition of public schools. And the final reason for limited supply is that *new* supply, new schools representing parents' hopes and aspirations, require some assured funding, absent in the face of EFM. So that we have in this case, as in countless others, many of which we will see when we discuss smoke screens used to prevent choice, the deliciously ironic, but very sad reality: we dare not move from the status quo's educational finance monopoly because it is so bad that it has produced conditions in which choice is too dangerous. It might actually have a negative impact on the destructive status quo!

None of these kinds of arguments, of course, would confront a genuinely free pursuit of the parental North Star, as described in chapter 1, in social circumstances unlike our own. But they do confront choice efforts in this country, and they help result in a very substantially mottled collection of choice efforts because each such effort has to answer not just the question of what should be done for parents' and students' sakes, but also has to answer all of the questions thrown up by those who, for whatever reason of self-interest or misguided altruism, want to defend the status quo. Thus instead of simply following the parental North Star to something like the four-step model described above in this volume or its equivalent shown in, for example, Denmark or Australia, the choice efforts in the United States are always digging out from under, trying to overcome the status quo and the arguments used to defend it.

Moreover, the path to school choice in the United States is not one path, as I indicated, but fifty paths. That is where education happens in the United States. It happens in the states. The federal structure is relatively unimportant to these questions. Its special pertinence is to serve exemplar purposes, and it rarely does that.

But even these speckled paths of the many states, arduous and bumpy as they are, are better than the sometimes illusory blind alleys that can beckon school choice people in the United States. I refer to such potentially blind alleys as public school-only choice and one variation thereof, the so-called charter school movement.

The charter school movement has considerable momentum in the United States. As of this writing, nineteen states have enacted charter legislation, and several others are on the brink. There is wide variety among the specific charter adaptations, particularly in the degree of independence charter schools can have from traditional monopoly controls. But generally speaking charter schools, though fully state-funded and chartered, operate with greater independence than traditional public schools, and are typically independent of local school districts. Charter schools are funded on a per-pupil basis, and their students (and parents) make an act of choice to attend. Usually, the charter school is designed to attract "special needs" students.

Precisely because they differ in these important respects from the often disastrous status quo, charter systems have generated a good bit of anticipation and excitement. I do not want to spoil anyone's fun, but it is necessary to introduce a few cautions and caveats. Remember the North Star: comprehensive parental freedom in education through school choice without financial penalty. That can only be achieved by dismantling educational finance monopoly (EFM); and replacing it with parental allocation of tax dollars to schools judged by parents to be most worthy for their children. That is a natural step because it makes parents' rights equal to their responsibilities. With such a North Star in mind, we can ask of every educational funding reform: does it advance us toward our goal? Does it advance us as far as we can and should advance? Does it have any potential for being a *misstep* which, however presented, might actually deter progress toward the true goal of parental freedom?

When such questions are asked of the charter movement, the answers must give us pause. I believe the fundamental fact is that "only in America," trapped as we are in EFM's destructive snares, and blinded as we are by EFM's smoke screens, would anyone think that charter schools were adequate or sufficient. Indeed, only in that suffering America would anyone even think of charters as a suitable device *apart from a true comprehensive choice system.*

Within a true choice system—where parents select schools, including religiously based schools, without financial penalty—charter schools would have the same rightful potential as any other educational offering.

Charter varieties would either succeed and survive, or fail and disappear, as would school offerings generally. Indeed, the more important question about charters within a choice system is whether the commercial ventures among them could survive, since they would have to compete not just against bloated monopoly schools as now but also against the already efficient independent ones. Who could quarrel with the idea of charter in an arena of true choice?

But as grafts on a continuing EFM; forced to exclude all religiously based schools; and tied entirely to pre-existing state funding mechanisms; the substantial limitations of charter systems are evident. As American experience and the experience of nations with true choice make abundantly clear, much of the parental motivation to choose alternate schools is religious and ethical. Thus, the greatest natural dynamic for encouraging choice, comparison, and competition in education is eliminated in the American charter movement.

There are other problems. Since they typically expect funding equivalent to the levels of monopoly-protected public schools, charters cannot provide immediate cost savings. Relatedly, they do not introduce cost competition to help achieve more rational educational budgeting. Depending on the specifics of state legislation, charters can turn out to be little more than another form of public school-only choice, and provide very few of true choice's benefits.

Such weaknesses as these do not mean charters necessarily should be opposed. If they can provide, on an interim basis, even limited help to some American children and parents trapped in an unsuccessful status quo, then they deserve support. They would merit active opposition, however, if they became occasions for delaying or diverting true choice. There are signs that some natural school choice supporters, including elements of the business community and some political leaders, have lost their focus when charters have been adopted. They appear to think that basic reform of EFM, and comprehensive growth of parental freedom, would somehow inevitably accompany charters. There is no such inevitability.

How to put it all summarily? Charters, if seen as, described as, and *made to be* an interim step toward comprehensive choice—Yes! Charters, if thought to be adequate or sufficient, or inadvertently permitted to put off true parental freedom—No!

The fact is that the charter movement can help impede, perhaps even destroy school choice if it is not used carefully and effectively. On the other side of the coin, we do want to note that in public school-only choice and in the charter version thereof there is one positive contribution they indisputably can make to the development of true school choice in this country. And that is that when the defenders of the status quo, the unions and professional educational bureaucratic structures, concede to even public school-only choice or charters, they are conceding one thing which they do not like to talk about but which is implicitly true in any case: that parents are able to do rational choosing of educational alternatives. This is a point worth noting, for one of the standard, though only whispered, arguments against true choice is that, "Well, how can we put it delicately— parents really cannot be trusted to choose well for their children."

Despite the fact that public school only-choice and charters have this one saving virtue, they remain for purposes of true school choice poten- tially destructive. They are perfectly representative of the mastery of the status quo. They are "poor substitutes" dictated by educational finance monopoly. They are not what would naturally occur if parents were free to form schools and respond to schools formed, such as in the nations described in chapter 6. Charters in such a situation would compete if they were able to compete; they would survive if they were able to survive, but they bring relatively little to the table if you have a genuine choice system.

So back to the efforts in the states to achieve true school choice and to avoid, or ensure the only-transitional status of, such potentially terminal side roads as public school only-choice and charters. The choice efforts in each state have to overcome the particular conditions of that state. The lead- ers have to make prudential judgments about what might work, how to get started. Thus, for example, in Wisconsin, a leader in school choice reform, we find the form of the reform being the expansion of the Milwaukee Pa- rental Choice Program (MPCP). Introduced by Wisconsin Representative Annette Polly Williams, the original MPCP was designed to allow 1000 low-income children to attend private, nonsectarian schools using vouch- ers worth either the private school's per pupil operating cost, or the state's per pupil aid to MPS, whichever was lower. In Wisconsin the central battle for school choice has been fought around the expansion of MPCP to in- clude religious schools and to increase the level of potential participation in that program. But still and all, MPCP expansion obviously is a limited, very modified choice effort. It is limited by very sharp means testing. It is limited even more obviously by geographical confines, and it is therefore in no sense a model for how to do school choice if one is free to think broadly and seriously about school choice vs. EFM. But it may *well* be a model for how to get school choice started in a given jurisdiction.

Similarly, if we look at Pennsylvania, another "hot spot" for contemporary school choice activities, we discover that the vehicle for school choice penetration and breakout in Pennsylvania, as pushed by Governor Tom Ridge in 1995 and as fashioned by the REACH Alliance and colleagues, was limited in other senses. It was potentially statewide and in that sense had far greater potential than MPCP expansion. But on the other side of the coin, it was much more sharply limited in terms of its financial potential. Pennsylvania's HB1640, supported by Governor Tom Ridge, would have spent $38,500,000 in state funds to implement a statewide voucher program which would have been phased-in over three years, with the poorest families qualifying first, and, later, families from all districts, for vouchers worth $700 for K-8 and $1000 for high school students. So, it was a crucially important venture. It would have been a legitimate snowball starting down the hill. It was, at the same time, a very far cry from true choice, obviously far short of any ideal of what a true choice system would look like. But both these efforts, Wisconsin's and Pennsylvania's, are admirable as ways to take the first step, to get started on the process of parental liberation.

We need to note, as well, in the context of how to do school choice in the fifty states, the particular problem of one step or two in states with constitutional impediments which make it necessary for a citizen referendum type activity, a constitutional modification, to precede the specific application of a school choice system within the state. The *Witters, Mueller,* and *Zobrest* Supreme Court decisions clearly affirm what reasonable people would expect: tuition support for children in sectarian schools, when parents are the conduits, does not violate First Amendment church-state provisions. The constitutions of many states have been interpreted as in conformity with federal practice on church and state, and in those states the natural and sufficient path to school choice is legislative action.

In some other states, however, one or another constitutional provision has been interpreted as barring legislative enactment of true school choice. In such states, the path to true choice calls for a constitutional change removing the impediment as well as the formation of a now-legitimate educational choice program. Even in the latter cases, such as California and Oregon, there remains another question that calls for serious deliberation. That question: is it better to try to amend the constitution and in the same action incorporate the specific school choice provision; or is it better simply to seek to amend the constitution so as to *authorize* school choice, and then define the specific form through the legislative process?

An operating principle for this writer: the school choice struggle will take different forms in different jurisdictions, and the triumph will take different forms, as well. In the same spirit, I do not presume that the "one step or two" question has a universal answer. But I do suggest that there are great difficulties attaching to the one-step solution, and certain palpable advantages in the two-step. The two-step remedy—amend the constitution so as to authorize true choice, followed by legislative enactment of a specific program—has at least these things in its favor: (1) it neutralizes to some degree the financial disadvantage school choice groups typically have when they confront the defenders of the status quo educational finance monopoly (EFM); (2) it makes much easier the crucial task of building and sustaining the political coalition necessary to overcome EFM; (3) it most properly reflects the fact that the first form of school choice is not likely to be the last—because we are imperfect creatures, and because we are likely to move to full choice through several gradual steps if that is possible, as part of being sensitive to the needs of those trapped in the status quo.

The status quo's EFM defends itself by manipulating social inertia. It does this through large, professional staff structures, working with educational union members and what I call their "altruistic corollaries," the PTAs, school boards, et al. EFM defenders have available very substantial funds. The advocates of choice, by contrast, tend to be less richly funded and minimally staffed. They do have two powerful advantages, however: they have the power of the argument entirely in their favor— there being no educational downside to school choice; and they have a potentially dominant electoral capacity if they can unite the "natural constituencies" of choice.

The best way to bring those constituencies together in lasting fashion is to create an organization under which they can all fit for the common purpose of breaking EFM and creating parental choice without financial penalty. Such an organization can provide reliable funding to support a professional staff effort to lead the fight for school choice. If that fight adopts the two-step approach, it will likely have productive effects. To begin with, it is easier to construct a majority coalition around the general principle of school choice than around any particular form. Common sense tells us that, but we know it, too, from viewing the discrepancy between public opinion polls done at the general level and voter results in California, Colorado, and Oregon when they were looking at specific instruments.

Another crucial part of successful coalition-building is ensuring that all of choice's constituencies—inner-city parents, taxpayers' organizations, ethically-concerned groups, business associations, and so on—have a chance to participate in and contribute their special views to the formation of the choice policy proposal, and that is more easily done in the relatively fluid environment of legislative give-and-take than in the once-and-for-all, long-before-the-fact framework of a constitutional referendum. Any flaw is greatly magnified if it cannot be easily repaired.

If the authorizing-only approach is better for building a majority, that very success also promises to convince politicians that there *is* widespread support for school choice, which will positively influence subsequent legislative deliberation. As to the legislative process, there are several reasons for imagining that, in many jurisdictions, it will be the best place for designing specific choice programs. The normally vast financial advantage of EFM is neutralized in legislative matters to some degree by limitations on pressure group expenditures. By contrast, that financial advantage is emphasized in mass media advertising buys aimed at the broad population, such as in referenda. At the same time, the legislative process can more easily take a gradualistic, several-step path to school choice, precisely because its very nature presumes a willingness constantly to perfect an always imperfect human device. And in this process it will tend to be most responsive to choice's constituencies.

Finally, one of EFM's traditionally most important strengths can, in the context of full-fledged political party combat, turn into a serious weakness. EFM has forged control relationships between educational unions and bureaucracies, on the one hand, and state legislatures and their committees, on the other. In many cases, these unions have been preponderantly devoted to supporting one party. In such circumstances, opposition parties literally owe those unions nothing. Indeed, they may be alienated from them. When such opposition parties, free of control, can build school choice into their platforms they have a powerful issue which, among other things, can be used to demonstrate their freedom from special interest. EFM's traditional cozy relations with one party can be a real liability in a newly competitive legislature.

"Getting it all done at once" is a perfectly understandable instinct. But getting it *done* is the genuine objective, and I have offered here some arguments that suggest that, when a state-level constitutional impediment exists, two steps are more likely to succeed than one. At the very least, the realities noted here might incline anyone thinking of a one-step approach to make the referendum result easily amendable. Absent that, any specific approach will be vulnerable to "what if the worst happens?" attacks.

If we put all these problems together, we begin to see why American educational choice programs are mottled, though admirable. They are a motley but entirely admirable collection of efforts. In shaping them, their authors are constantly attempting to pull the teeth of the countless smoke screen critiques that EFM defenders bring to bear. The authors are constantly trying to anticipate the primary concerns that citizens and politicians will have and to meet those concerns in the shaping of the specific choice legislation. Naturally, therefore, any given choice legislation will vary substantially state to state, and it will always have certain homely and odd characteristics reflecting the conditions within that given jurisdiction. Thus, how to manage up-front costs, for example; how to provide special help for economically disadvantaged and special education children; how to avoid a windfall to the well off; how to ensure that the status quo does not lose dollars even if it *should* lose dollars; these are the kinds of things that the authors of state level school choice efforts have had to try to deal with as they have tried to launch, tried to get started the choice effort in their place.

But through all such struggles, lessons have been learned; the scars have led to strengthening rather than to weakening of the school choice efforts and there are model proposals which have evolved through these difficult circumstances. Presuming that there is no state level constitutional impediment in the jurisdiction under consideration, or that if there were it has been fixed by a limited referendum, then it can be seen how the following model handles the usual impediments and at the same time moves firmly toward the North Star of genuine parental freedom through school choice without financial penalty.

During the winter of 1994–95, Speaker of the U.S. House of Representatives Newt Gingrich became convinced that the children of the District of Columbia, under Congressional jurisdiction, were being horribly served by the educational status quo. He also believed that school choice should be part of the resolution to this crisis. At end-January, 1995, he asked various leaders of school choice efforts to offer counsel, and one of his counselors asked me to participate in the process.

In response to this initiative, I decided to provide a model bill which, though not designed for the District in any particular sense, could help inform Congressional leadership as to the *general* characteristics of what a school choice program might look like. They and their aides and counselors could apply whatever special application and particulars seemed compelling to them.

For this purpose, I simply took one of the many excellent proposals that have been developed and revised and streamlined it. The particular legislation I used to shape a D.C. model was that of former Florida legislator Tom Feeney. The draft D.C. model is reproduced here for two reasons: first, to show the ease with which school choice *could* be brought to American jurisdictions if enlightened political action is possible. Second, with this concise model, I hope to give readers a "hands-on" sense of the issue and its potentials.

H.R. _____ A Bill to Improve all Education, Independent and Governmental, in the District of Columbia by Expanding Parents' Rights to School Choice Without Financial Penalty. This Will Be Accomplished by Creating the District of Columbia Tuition Scholarship Program.

Section 1. This act shall be known as the "District of Columbia Parental Choice in Education Act of 1995." It is the purpose of this act to establish a District-wide program empowering parents and guardians to exercise choice in the selection of schools for their children, thereby enhancing parental rights and encouraging comparison and competition among educational providers. This will benefit all students and schools. (See the 'Commentary' following this draft.)

Section 2. As used in this act:

(1) "Parent" means the natural or adoptive parent or legal guardian of a dependent child.

(2) "Participating school" means a public or private school located in the District that enters into an agreement with the District school authorities in accordance with the provisions of section 5. [Portability beyond District confines is an option well worth considering.]

(3) "Private school" means a school that is not maintained with public funds, that charges tuition or fees for the services it provides, and that is in compliance with the laws of the District.

(4) "Public school" means a school that is administered by a public governmental agency.

(5) "Resident school district" means a geographical area surrounding a public school from which students are assigned.

(6) "School" means a school that is authorized to provide elementary and/or secondary education under District law.

(7) "Eligible private school" means:

(a) A private school which has been operating for at least 2 years and meets standards pursuant to section 6; or

(b) A private school operating for less than 2 years which meets standards pursuant to section 6 and obtains a letter of credit or bond for one-third of the total amount of funds to be received through acceptance of certificates provided for in this act. The letter of credit or bond shall, in the event of nonperformance, be payable to the district school board.

Section 3. In order to achieve the purpose described in section 1, the District school authorities shall initiate and carry out a program in which the parent of each school-age child receives from the district school board, on request, a certificate that may be used for educational services at a participating school selected by the child's parent in accordance with the provisions of this act.

Section 4. (1) Each public school in the District shall become a participating school. The responsible officials for each eligible private school shall decide whether that school shall become a participating school.

(2) Subject to the provisions of subsection (3), a participating school shall admit children with certificates who apply, up to the limit of the school's capacity, after reserving places for children admitted in accordance with the school's regular admissions practices.

(3)(a) A participating school shall establish criteria for the admission of children with certificates that are consistent with the admissions criteria that it regularly applies.

(b) In the case of a participating public school, the District school authorities shall establish criteria for the equitable allocation of places for children with certificates if there are insufficient places to serve all such children requesting such places.

Section 5. A participating school shall enter into an agreement with the District school authorities. Such agreement shall provide that the participating school shall furnish a child who is accepted in the school and who tenders a certificate under the provisions of this act, and, if applicable, a supplementary tuition payment required to satisfy any remainder of a participating school's tuition, an education equivalent to that provided to all other children in the school. All or part of the funds for such supplementary tuition payment may be secured from the individual student's personal education account established pursuant to section 14. Such agreement shall also provide that the participating school shall meet the standards listed in section 6. Schools that agree to meet the standards listed in section 7 shall be certified as participating schools.

Section 6. Certificates may be redeemed at participating schools which:

(1) Have admission policies which do not discriminate as to race, ethnicity, national origin, or sex.

(2) Provide a curriculum which includes five core subjects: English, including reading fundamentals for elementary school students; mathematics; science; history; and geography.

(3) Meet minimum health and safety standards with which private schools must currently comply.

(4) Disclose teacher credentials to parents.

(5) Report student achievement data as measured by standardized tests or other criteria as determined by the pertinent District authorities.

(6) Provide to the District's Choice Information Center information regarding:

(a) Its participation in the certificate program.

(b) Its program of instruction, educational philosophy, and particular purpose.

(c) Achievement data regarding students attending the school, which data may be stated in the aggregate.

(d) The incidence of illegal drug use.

(e) School discipline and safety.

Section 7. Participating schools, regardless of size, shall be accorded maximum flexibility to educate their students and shall be free from unnecessary, burdensome, onerous regulation. No regulation of private schools beyond that required by this act and that which applied to private schools on January 1, 1995, shall be issued or enacted unless approved by a three-fourths vote of the Legislature. In any legal proceeding challenging a regulation as inconsistent with the provisions of this section, the governmental body issuing or enacting the regulation shall have the burden of establishing that the regulation is essential to assure the health, safety, or education of students, or, as to any land use regulation, that the governmental body has a compelling interest in issuing or enacting it; does not unduly burden or impede private schools or the parents of students therein; and will not harass, injure, or suppress private schools.

Section 8. Certificates are grants-of-aid to children through their parents, not to the schools in which the children are enrolled. The selection of parents of a school shall not constitute a decision or act of the state or any of its subdivisions. Payment to a religious or parochial school for educational services under this act shall not constitute aid to any church, sect, religious denomination, or sectarian institution.

Section 9. A parent of a child with a certificate may use the certificate for educational services at a participating school only if the child is admitted to the participating school.

Section 10. The value of a certificate, for any individual student, shall be set at 75% of the Districts per pupil expenditure at the appropriate level, but no certificate may be redeemed for more than the amount of the tuition and fees regularly charged by the participating school providing the educational services.

Section 11. (1) The purpose of this section is to grant to low-income families an equal opportunity of educational choices by making private schools a feasible option.

(2) Any student in kindergarten through grade 12 who is eligible to participate in the free lunch program, pursuant to 42 USC 1758(b), or is a low-income student pursuant to a subsequent definition of low-income student as may be adopted by the Legislature, shall be an eligible low-income student, entitled to the enhanced tuition allowances as set forth in section 13(2)(b).

Section 12. (1) The District school authorities shall establish and maintain a Choice Information Center to provide information and assistance to parents in selecting a school. The Choice Information Center shall provide information on all participating schools and shall include all information obtained pursuant to section 6(6).

(2) The District school authorities shall publish and make available to all parents a list of all participating schools.

Section 13. A parent of a child with a certificate shall present the certificate to the participating school that the child attends. The participating school shall present the certificate for payment or redemption to the District school authorities.

(1)(a) A participating public school shall receive, in addition to its regular budget, funds equal to the full value of a certificate for each student who transfers into the respective participating public school upon presentation of such certificates to the district school board.

(b) A participating public school shall lose funds equal to the full value of a certificate for each resident school district student who transfers from the respective participating public school.

(2) A participating private school shall receive funds equal to a percentage of the full value of a certificate, as set forth in this subjection, for each certificate presented by the respective participating private school.

(a) For the first school year after the effective date of this act, participating private schools shall receive 60 percent of the full value of a certificate, pursuant to section 10, for each certificate presented by the respective participating private school. Each subsequent year, the percentage of the full value of a certificate received by a participating private school, pursuant to section 10, for each certificate presented shall increase 10 percent, that is, 70 percent, 80 percent, 90 percent, until the percentage equals 100 percent.

(b) For the first 3 years after the effective date of this act, a participating private school shall receive 100 percent of the full value of a certificate, pursuant to section 10, for the redemption of each certificate tendered by an eligible low-income student, pursuant to section 11(2). Each subsequent year, the percentage of the full value of a certificate, pursuant to section 10, received by a participating private school for the redemption of each certificate tendered by an eligible low-income student, pursuant to section 11(2), shall increase 10 percent, that is, 110 percent, 120 percent, until the percentage equals 120 percent.

Section 14. In the event that a participating private school charges tuition less than the maximum certificate value for each individual student, the District school authorities shall hold the balance of the certificate value amount in a personal education account in that student's name, to be used to supplement later kindergarten through grade 12 tuition or to defray the cost of postsecondary education. On the student's 26th birthday, any funds remaining in the student's account shall revert to the general funds of the District's school authorities.

Section 15. This act shall take effect _____.

I appended to this D.C. draft proposal a simple commentary which highlights some of its approaches, and that commentary follows.

The proposed Act, adapted from Tom Feeney's Florida proposal, is informed by the debates and battles which have arisen over school choice. In particular, it builds in antidotes to the major smoke screens used by the defenders of the status quo to combat parents' rights. Several of the more important points can be noted here.

1. It directly challenges allegations of church-state entanglement by highlighting the simple truth: this aims to aid *parents*, not churches, not even schools.
2. It directly challenges the common smear against parents—"how can *they* judge schools?"—by providing a clear choice information program.
3. It is sensitive to low-income and special education needs.
4. It provides a graduated transition period, providing the schools and structure of the *status quo* time for adjustment to the new world.
5. It builds in a strong incentive for the schools to restrain costs by establishing student educational "savings accounts," which is a strong incentive to parents to look for efficient and economical education delivery.
6. It protects the independent schools from new and undue intrusion by political authorities.
7. It provides dollar values sufficient to purchase most extant independent education *and* to invite new supply of such education. Average tuition at D.C. Catholic elementary schools, for example, is $1940.00, and average secondary tuition was $6583.00. (Report of the Archdiocese of Washington for 1994–95.)

Thus, even with our many and different jurisdictions; and the very heavy burdens that history has placed on the school choice effort; and the power with which the status quo is defended by educational finance monopoly defenders; there are relatively simple approaches which meet all substantial objections and can provide genuine choice to parents. Relatively simple, I have said, but not easy. And why is it not easy? Why cannot the simple, right, and overwhelmingly agreeable objective of parental freedom be achieved more easily than it has been possible to achieve it in the United States? The next four chapters will provide answers to those questions.

Part III

Then, Why Not Here, Now?

8

Why Are We in a Quagmire?
I: Historical Accidents, Social Inertia,
and Political Frustration

In chapter 7 we argued that it would be possible to have school choice without financial penalty in the United States simply, though not easily. This chapter's concern, the question of why we do not have it, I am convinced is answered neither simply *nor* easily. But the question of why we do not have that which we so obviously deserve, that which America's parents and children especially so obviously deserve, is *the* question, clearly. Is not the nation, and are not the states, democratic? Are not the people wise enough to see what is right, and free enough to achieve it? "Quagmire," indeed!

We have the policies we have, and we are in the quagmire that we have here described, because of historical accidents and the theory of the common school which motivated certain shapers of American educational policy in the nineteenth century. Historical accidents and that intentionality, along with some anti-Catholicism, led to educational finance monopoly (EFM). (See, e.g., Charles Glenn, *The Myth of the Common School*, Amherst, Massachusetts, 1987.) Other historical accidents kept educational finance monopoly in place, until its roots became deeply set; then it became self-perpetuating; and, by the middle of the twentieth century, Americans found themselves in the grip of social inertia, and that social inertia was and is available to be manipulated by those interested in maintaining the educational finance monopoly. (An earlier form of this summary of how our imprisoning status quo evolved in history can be found in my "The Family's Values and Educational Choice," *The Family in America*, March, 1993, vol. 7., no. 3.)

A few years ago, a very good and very bright friend, whose public schooling concluded shortly before World War II, placed the issue exactly right: "Gee, whatever happened to the public schools? They were all right when I was a kid." This implicit question is a crucial part of the inertia which sustains the status quo, and a crucial common attitude used by the vested interest defenders of that status quo. It reflects the fact that for much of our modern history the public schools seemed to work well enough, and the memories of those old enough to think back forty or fifty years are by and large positive ones. Since the system of monopoly financing which supported those schools and denied funding to independent alternatives was essentially the same then as now, how can I (or anyone) identify that system as the root of the problem? That part of the educational equation has not changed. If the schools are markedly less successful than before must not other factors have done the foul deed? This critique of my criticism is quite understandable, and worthy of serious examination.

The perverse character of EFM was potentially as real fifty years ago as it is today. Such a system inevitably tends to produce effects characteristic of monopoly: bloated operation, inefficient use of funds, nonresponsiveness to consumers, organizational self-servingness and circular evaluation, proliferation of secondary and tertiary programs and personnel. But such natural and notorious results of this mechanism were for a long time subdued in American education, because of various accidental and transitory, but momentarily decisive, social conditions. In comparative politics there is a useful distinction made between "fair weather" and "foul weather" conditions in which political structures are tested. This refers to such factors as social and ethnic harmony or discord, economic strength or weakness, geopolitical security or vulnerability, and the like. It is obvious that if enough "fair weather" social conditions exist, the political structure will not be severely tested. But when the weather turns foul, the test comes and poor systems fail.

So it is on our topic. America's EFM sailed in fair weather for many decades and its drastic and innate shortcomings were not exposed. Let us note some of the more important of these fortuitous circumstances — and their transitoriness. One of the most important is this: public education was traditionally essentially local, even down to neighborhoods, and the local communities were greatly homogeneous. Local control of local schools resting on greatly homogeneous communities meant, among other things, that those schools possessed common and shared values and behavioral norms and expectations. These school policies were naturally reinforced by the families the policies reflected. Such an ethical community existed and expressed itself naturally, and easily fended off the ethical drift and vacuum so characteristic of today's public schools. This obviously was a time before today's extreme litigiousness and judicially enforced elevation of individuality over community values.

A greatly ironic event also occurred in that happier history. The Catholic community was the primary "sore thumb" in yesterday's American ethical homogeneity. Indeed, the late-nineteenth century Catholic community saw that cultural homogeneity, as it defined the public schools, for what it was: an essentially Protestant ethic giving implicit shape and direction to America's public education. That insight in the late nineteenth century and extending into the twentieth gave rise to much Roman Catholic discontent with prevailing realities, and this was a clear omen of the agonies to come under the system of finance monopoly. But instead of being confined to a public system increasingly bothersome to them, chafing and building steam that might have led to more pluralistic funding designs, a la Europe, Roman Catholics were given an essentially cost-free outlet. The tremendous magnanimity of the nuns and others within the Church community created a whole other system and offered it to Roman Catholics. Indeed, the nuns gave the Roman Catholics their own system of educational choice before anyone used the term, before anyone knew school choice policies would later be required to break the destructive tendencies of EFM. Choice was privately given to Roman Catholics and greatly used by them, and it did exactly what choice can do: it gave parents freedom and control in determining their childrens' educational environment, and it removed the financial penalty for choosing an independent school (the essential choice mechanism); it produced what is now seen to have been and still is an extraordinarily effective educational method; and, momentarily, it saved the public schools from one of the worst results of EFM: it protected them for awhile from having to adopt the least-common-denominator (l-c-d) moral face which, in turn, becomes a vacuum.

This Roman Catholic opt out, in which the essentially nonremunerated religious gave Catholics an effective system of educational choice, is highly important for yet another reason. It helps give the lie to the claim that "choice is just experimental" and not to be trusted until "some time" it goes through a never-ending series of tests (each of which in turn will be fought and deemed inadequate by vested interests opposed to choice).

Our own vast and successful experience with choice gives it the green light, and if we add the relevant experience of other nations that take choice for granted, such as those examined in chapter 6, we see what is clearly true: the tag of "just experimental" is, truly, just a smoke screen, one of many. This smoke screen aspect of the school choice struggle in America will be examined more thoroughly in chapter 10.

But the homogeneity that once permitted the public schools to provide a solid ethical content is gone in large parts of the nation, and in every major city. Even where it exists, in small communities, for example, the intrusive extension of court decisions elevating individual prerogatives over community standards has weakened the capacity of any community to insure that its public schools will reflect an acceptable community norm. Local control has been eroded in this way. The corollary growth of professional bureaucracies, educational unions, and state educational structures further contributed to school inability to reflect and articulate a consensus of parental and community values. This is the apparent explanation for the increasing incidence of conflict over local school board elections, featuring various efforts by parents' groups to take back the destinies of local schools.

A remarkably apt summary of the remoteness and nonresponsive character of contemporary public schools is contained in an article by John E. Chubb and Terry M. Moe entitled "Politics, Markets, and the Organization of Schools" (*American Political Science Review*, vol. 82, no. 4, December, 1988). Thus, at p. 1067, concerning the separation of public schools from parental control: "The proper constituency of even a single public school is a huge and heterogeneous one whose interests are variously represented by formally prescribed agents, politicians and administrators, at all levels of government. Parents and students, therefore, are but a small part of the legitimate constituency of 'their own' schools. The schools are not meant to be theirs to control and are literally not supposed to provide the kind of education they might want." Private schools, on the other hand, must be responsive precisely to the market of parents' desires for their children. Thus, a smaller and more homogeneous ruling constituency naturally exists in private schools, and can expect responsible school performance. The public schools often are essentially autonomous, exactly as one expects in monopolistic conditions. The parents do not control, as seen above; even the electorate does not control, for the elected boards are not in a dialectical relationship with anyone, but instead typically become spear carriers for educational bureaucrats and unions; state departments of education become collaborators and champions; and state legislators are prone to be captured in committee by persevering and well-financed educational bureaucrats and unions. So the normal countervailing power—argument, dialectic, win-lose, in office-out of office—does not apply. It is that fact which spawns the *symptoms* which preoccupy and inflame so many. The *cause* which most miss is EFM.

Yet another of the old accidents that gave America's public schools such fair weather in which to sail for so long was the fact of American economic independence, and, later, dominance. Until the Great Depression, America was not much tested by external realities. It prospered under prevailing geopolitical conditions—weak neighbors to the north and south, fish to the east and west, as the old joke had it—and under a highly unusual degree of economic autonomy. Though the Depression introduced us a bit to the interconnectedness of things, and World War II ended our isolation forever, we emerged from the latter so economically dominant that, even though we knew we were now inextricably connected with the world beyond our shores, we were not economically tested for twenty years after World War II. Though our educational system was actually beginning to develop the malfunctions for which it is now storied, its products—the educated young—were also not tested as they are in today's extremely competitive international conditions, where work force quality is inevitably under scrutiny, and increasingly found wanting. This is another illustration of fair weather artificially protecting the public schools from the results of EFM.

Confusing Ends and Means

One of the basic reasons why this sad situation has been tolerated up to now is what I refer to as the ends-means confusion in understanding contemporary education. When one of many alternative means to a given end comes to be thought of as if it were the end itself, the confused party is in an essentially irrational situation. Not just irrational, either: it is also irredeemable until the victim crashes out of that mesmerized condition. For a means to an end (public schools as a means to educational achievement for persons and society, for example) can be measured, compared, and assessed. How well does it work, compared to other means available, in achieving the various objectives set for it? But let the means come to be seen as the end and ruin beckons. The good end of education for youth and society cannot itself be criticized. Thus if one comes to think of one means as identical with the end itself, then the means can no longer be assessed rationally.

And to a large extent that has occurred in the U.S. The "public schools" have come to be spoken of as the equivalent of education by many people. And the many good souls who want to help "education" too often start out by imagining that that means "helping public schools"—even though those schools, artificially protected by EFM, are in many ways symptoms of the problem, not solutions for it. When Wisconsin Governor Tommy G. Thompson decided Wisconsin's educational offerings needed reform in 1995, he did not just propose expansion of the Milwaukee Parental Choice Program to include more students and religious schools, thereby insuring the mainland's first true choice program. He also and at the same time moved to replace the "Department of Public Instruction" with a new "Department of Education"—a symbolically important stripping of a *means* of its *end-in-itself* status. Any serious dedication to improving educational performance in the U.S. really must begin by making a rigorous resolve never to view any schooling alternative, public or private, as an end in itself but just as a means to the good end of educational achievement for persons' and society's sakes. The comparison and competition that are possible when there are many recognized means to the end are simply unavailable, and are replaced by an irrational context, if one means is treated as if it were the end itself. Ends-means confusion is, in many respects, the ultimate victory of EFM's defenders employing social inertia, and the ultimate challenge confronting school choice advocates.

To illustrate the general impact of social inertia, and the specific importance of confusing ends and means, it will be worthwhile to examine the recent case of Ambassador Walter Annenberg's $500,000,000.00 effort to help America's public schools. Can a half-billion dollar gift to public K-12 education greatly help bring peace to American schools? Or is it likely to be lost in the same futile black hole that devours most American "reform" efforts?

In the movie *Blazing Saddles*, Mel Brooks' spoof of every Western ever made, there is an amusingly graphic portrayal of self-imposed futility. For individuals it illustrates what happens when we surrender our minds to our habits. Applied to society, it suggests how social inertia can block serious reform. In this particular sketch the gang of bad guys is riding hell-bent to raid the little town in which at least some virtue still resides. To delay the gang long enough to permit the town to defend itself, the good guys put a toll booth on the trail the gang is following. Despite the fact that the booth stands alone, with no fence, and with clear space to travel on either side, the bad guys halt, keep their horses in check, and wait impatiently for the slow and destructive-for-their-purposes process of toll-paying.

That is a good bit like most Americans when they see the need for educational reform. Though good guys, not bad, they are trapped behind unlocked doors, endlessly chasing the symptoms of education's illness. They are conditioned to stop short of looking at a prime cause, educational finance monopoly. Most American educational reformers are EFM's captives—but can be free whenever they wish. All they need do is focus on education, rather than public education, on the *end* rather than the *means*. Then they will see that in a free society many educational forms naturally evolve, that parents can best judge their particular quality for their own children, and that funding should follow parents' choice. As soon as they do that, the door will open and serious reform will become possible.

When Ambassador Walter Annenberg's monumental 1993 $500,000,000.00 gift to American education was announced, it appeared to be a classic casualty of self-enforced captivity to EFM. There is great and understandable anguish over growing violence in America's public schools. There is corollary interest in learning how to control such behavior and increase the level of calm in these schools. Ambassador Annenberg's gift to K-12 education was greatly motivated by concerns for the safety of America's young people in public schools, and we applaud such motives, naturally. (See the announcement in the *New York Times*, December 17, 1993.)

However, it is possible that much of Americans' attention to school violence is misdirected and will be unavailing if it focuses only on this question: how can we restore safety to our public schools? That is an understandable and legitimate question, but it leaves unasked even better ones: if free to choose, what parents would select schools known to be relatively unsafe? Answer: none. If to be choiceworthy they had to maintain discipline, demand self-control, insist on a safe, secure, and tranquil environment, how many schools would work to ensure such conditions? Answer: every one of them, including public schools, and those that did not succeed would close.

The atmosphere of violence and fear that apparently was most compelling to Mr. Annenberg when he made his announcement is itself symptomatic of the problems which have developed within the structure of American public education, sheltered (and victimized) as it is by educational finance monopoly. While this has nothing to do with public schools as such, it has much to do with the monopolistic environment in which those schools have been made to operate. The problem of failed safety is only one of many expressions of American educational malaise ranging from family alienation from imposed schools, to excessive cost, to irrational budgeting modalities, to poor educational performance in terms of standardized test achievements, and to a general disorientation and self-servingness within a system that is supposed to be serving human needs outside itself.

The problem of school-centered violence is in no sense a surprising phenomenon if one understands the causal context out of which it emerges. Since Mr. Annenberg's gift was dedicated essentially to monopoly-protected schools, that may mean he did not realize that the monopoly structure itself may be a substantial, perhaps even determining factor behind the violence in those schools. He clearly hoped and expected that his money, mixed with matching money and poured into the enormous maw that is public education funding in this country, would have some sort of substantial impact. There is no reason to imagine such an outcome. The fundamental fact is that the symptom he trained his attention on is one of many traceable in substantial part to the common source of monopolistic environment for education. That environment tends to remove from itself the normal restraining influences of parental control and family-engendered self-restraints that children bring with them. Such interiorized values, if reinforced by the educational environment, are the ingredients of conscience that, under natural circumstances, help youngsters differentiate between good and bad actions, acceptable and unacceptable behavior. But, as we saw in chapter 3, monopoly-protected, one-size-fits-all schools cannot provide the specific moral reinforcement that encourages self-restraint and communal tranquillity by reminding youngsters of who they are, where they come from, what is expected of them, and who is waiting at home. Prohibited from providing specific and pointed ethical frameworks and foundations, EFM's schools are reduced to an ethic of the lowest common denominator. That, in turn, results in a normative vacuum for purposes of instruction and behavior, and such vacuums are filled by the latest secular trends. Such vacuums, at the same time, invite egocentric and excessive behavior from the young people caught in them.

But if this is so obvious, why did not Mr. Annenberg, and why do not people generally, move against the cause? Why do they not free themselves from the captivity of a system that, in fact, tends to generate the very symptoms they rebel against? The general answer to that general question is social inertia. As we noted above, the status quo in terms of educational funding, EFM, is inherited from an earlier, much more homogeneous time in which its ruinous effects were muted and seldom seen because of various transitory "fair weather" conditions in the U.S. EFM is a long-standing policy and it is, in fact, a habit of American society. The public schools that materially benefit from it are themselves objects of nostalgic memory for many people in America, particularly older people. This system then brings into itself such persons as PTA volunteers and other parents' and civic groups who are likely to see themselves as well-disposed, altruistic agents of the good, doing good things because, after all, they are "helping the kids." While we should welcome such altruism, we must remind ourselves that a truly good action requires a discriminating choice of the means as well as an enlightened motivation.

In addition to benefiting from long habits and misguided good intentions, EFM is sustained by traditional American insularity. We are inclined to presume that God is on our side and that if something has been done here for any length of time, it probably is the right thing to do. This attitude inevitably reinforces the status quo and adds to social inertia on educational funding policy. All such elements of social inertia are then seized upon and reinforced by the extremely powerful and well-financed vested interests that benefit from the status quo and EFM. These vested interests chant such mantras as the myth of the common school and the other standard smoke screens aimed at creating moral doubt about anyone who suggests that educational finance monopoly should be broken.

Those who benefit materially from the status quo do all within their power, quite naturally, not surprisingly, nor with evil intention, to get people to think of a specific *means*—public schools protected by educational finance monopoly—as if it were the *end* of educational policy. To the extent they are successful, then all the forces of social inertia are employed to entangle those who are concerned about the quality of American education in a snare in which fundamental change, change of the causal categories, is discouraged and all change efforts are trained on symptoms.

That which most needs changing is by this process transformed into something sacrosanct and untouchable, as Americans are conditioned to believe any tampering with EFM is equivalent to an attack on public schools and the welfare of children. Thus, for example, Mr. Annenberg may have been caught in one of those traps. There is little in the statements surrounding his grant to suggest that he or his advisors freed themselves of the funding status quo and asked themselves whether or not there are basic causal changes which perhaps should be considered. They may well not have seen the formative power of EFM, nor of the major funding alternative: parental choice of schools. Instead, they seemed quite prepared to deal with EFM's symptoms, thus setting out to reform *within* a causal system the very nature of which works against their efforts and sets them on a never-ending and basically unproductive path. By contrast, if he had looked at the relative peacefulness of *chosen* independent schools, poor and rich, suburban and inner city, where family and school reinforce each other regarding behavioral expectations, Mr. Annenberg might have found that the model of tranquillity already existed and did not need to be reinvented, but only to be propagated by choice-encouraging funding methods.

What is needed to overcome such captivity, of course, is to help those who are distressed by the *symptoms* of educational failure to recognize the *causes*, as well, and then to realize that they are themselves the natural constituencies which can bring about fundamental reform of American education if they will but develop their political potential and join other constituencies to forge a decisive political force.

This would help them see that many of the symptoms that concern them have a cause, that the cause is monopoly in educational funding, and that the cause can be eradicated. If this cause is eradicated, the first and primary beneficiaries, as we saw in chapter 6, will be the public schools themselves, which will prosper educationally in an environment of normal human incentive to excel, an environment of choice in which success means making yourself choiceworthy. In a genuine choice system, attendance at public schools would be an act of choice just as much as is attendance at an independent school. That act of choosing public or private creates the "moral contract" between home and school that is missing in a monopoly environment. But to achieve comprehensive choice will require great labor because the vested interests do have social inertia to exploit, and these vested interests are themselves strong and professionally adept at the work they are about—namely, maintaining the status quo against all critics. Until we commit to work "for the duration" for this most fundamental change, we are rather like Mel Brooks' zanies, sitting impatiently but impotently behind the unlocked door of educational finance monopoly. The alternative is to open the door, remove EFM, enact educational choice, empower parents to select their child's school, and permit the natural dynamics of a free educational environment to treat both cause and symptoms of America's educational difficulties.

As we saw above, American education freed of EFM would not be satisfied with this question: How can we restore peace and safety in America's public schools? That is not a bad question, but freed of EFM, the more likely and better question would be: What parents in their right mind would *choose* a school judged to be unsafe? Answer: none. And the next question: If all schools had to make themselves choice worthy, how would they do so? Answer: by convincing parents that they were good for their children, including, obviously, *safe* for their children. Mr. Annenberg might have done more for the good objective of tranquil educational conditions for American students if he had asked whether any educational providers (the means) already *had* a successful formula for creating peaceful schools and strong educational results (the end).

Political Frustration vs. "In It for the Duration"

The essential reason for dwelling on the results of historical accidents, and the corresponding social inertia that those accidents created, is not idle curiosity. It is not even pursuit of historicity. The essential reason for dwelling on that issue is that, without a firm grasp of what happened and the "uphill battle" it produced for school choice in the United States, there is no way to grasp the requirements of political action necessary to produce political change. Thus, a student of school choice in the United States encounters and has to understand the phenomenon of people seeing the abstract absurdity of the status quo and of people seeing the abstract beauty of school choice without financial penalty and transforming this clarity into too-easy political expectations. That, of course, is not the way political change of deeply rooted policy occurs. As a result, those who imagine that the issue is essentially a conceptual one have suffered extreme frustrations when their political efforts have failed. And, interestingly enough, such failures have become a new source of doubt, as we have seen people, choice advocates, suffer early defeat and begin to doubt whether or not the reality that they saw so clearly was truly true. These kinds of doubts come not from inadequacies of school choice theory, but from failure of political preparation and will and the sense of "in it for the duration" which is the necessary companion of any dedication to achieving school choice. There is no inadequacy in the essence of school choice, to be perfectly frank. It does not have an educational down side, as I often say. But there is a political hill that is higher than many choice advocates realized when they became devotees of that theory, and that, in turn, can produce an enervating frustration. When it is mistakenly imagined to be an end in itself, EFM is beyond question and criticism, and those who do question it and urge consideration of choice are confronted with essentially circular smoke screens in response. The standard list of smoke screens thrown up against educational choice is replete with assertions which make no sense whatsoever unless one begins with the presumption noted above: whatever we do, we must *not* disturb the fundamental monopolistic funding mechanism.

A couple of illustrations will establish the point. "Choice will siphon resources from public schools, already short of cash." This presupposes what is not known: how much money it takes to buy high quality education, of course. But, far worse, it rests on the presumption that monopoly-protected public schools—rather than the education of children—have a *right* to a certain amount of public money. That puts the means above the end, the cart before the horse, and makes evaluation impossible. Again: "Choice will mean taking public money from public schools and giving it to private, even religious schools." Not only is this false—choice provides support to *parents*, not schools, and the parents decide where to assign it with absolutely no church-state entanglement—it is, also, another perfect illustration of circular thinking. It is entirely illogical—unless one begins with the presumption that the schools protected by EFM have a *right* to all public dollars which, again, makes them impossible to evaluate.

These and other smoke screens are superficially attractive, of course, or they would not serve their smoke screen purposes. But under analysis they have no logical power, for they are seen to be purely circular, as if one were to say, "this must be preserved because this must be preserved." That is the effect of social inertia.

Having seen the powerful natural sustaining capacity of social policy that has been in place long enough to have inertia working for it, we want now to add to the mix a very strong, very well-financed, very experienced group of defenders of the status quo. We will look at these people in more detail in the next chapter, but now we need only to note that they are defenders of vested interest, with substantial material benefits connected to maintaining the status quo. These people, interested in maintaining the status quo, do not start from zero in building a strategy of maintenance. Rather, they start with the massive reality of social inertia that is there for them to exploit and manipulate. In particular, it permits them to perpetuate and deepen the ends-means confusion noted above. Those who see the excellence of educational choice as an alternative to educational finance monopoly simply do not comprehend the depth of their problem unless they see the power in this combination of social inertia plus skilled and deep-pocketed and professional maintainers of the status quo. If seen, then no one who advocates choice will imagine that its achievement can be easy or quick.

In order to succeed, political strategy in favor of school choice requires a deep understanding of why we are stuck in the quagmire we are in. It requires a deep appreciation of what I have called social inertia. Devotees of school choice, if they want to avoid enthusiasm-killing frustration, must realize that even an egregiously bad policy will not change by itself. Social inertia sees to that. But educational finance monopoly and the structures that it creates around it have fruits that are sufficiently bad, and have provoked sufficient criticism that we can safely say they would not have withstood change so well and so long just because of social inertia. Educational finance monopoly has withstood change up to now because that same social inertia has been effectively used by forces who want educational finance monopoly to remain the essence of the status quo. Who are these people, and why do they work for the continuance of such a poor policy? We will examine them, and their apparent motivation, in chapter 9.

9

Why Are We in a Quagmire?
II: Who Would Do Such A Thing?

A policy, and its associated structures, whose symptoms are so roundly criticized would not and could not sustain itself in a democratic environment if it did not have very substantial and very effective enforcement and encouragement coming from well-placed people. But if the policy and structures in question are as humanly destructive as I am here suggesting, then who would work to maintain them? Who would be so oblivious to society's needs, and do such a very bad thing?

Again, the answer to those questions is not a story of "bad guys versus good guys." The story here being told is the story of bad policy, which has spawned implementing structures and which, taken together, constitute what I refer to as educational finance monopoly or EFM. These structures are conduits for dollars, very large dollars; so that the essential nature of the beast, looked at from EFM's perspective, becomes the search for political control to guarantee financial advantage. Groups of people have direct material benefit flowing from the status quo funding method, EFM. There is nothing surprising about people defending such a status quo. It does not make them evil, but it does not make their position objectively convincing, either. Here we want to note, also, that if I have described the objective of EFM's defenders correctly, namely to maintain control over finance monopoly, and if parental allocation of some or all of tax dollars dedicated to education is the primary alternative to EFM, then those who are the material beneficiaries of EFM, if confined to the simple truth, would have to praise monopoly and/or depreciate parents' capacity to choose wisely in order to defend their present situation. It is small wonder, given those two alternatives, that they tend to choose instead to make other kinds of sounds, the sounds of red herrings falling across the path to genuine reform.

So, the first and most important of the answers to the question of who would do such a thing is that all those people whose material welfare is, or is thought to be (and there is a real distinction here) tied to the EFM status quo can be expected to, and in fact do, provide the primary support for the maintenance of the status quo. I am talking about all public school personnel. I am talking about the unions to which most of those personnel belong. And, by the way, concerning the unions, I am again not talking about "bad guys versus good guys." Neither am I talking about unions generally, as if they were an unacceptable or even questionable element of social existence. But the thing about unions in the context of our discussion is that they operate in an often unchallenged, essentially nondialectical environment. This is quite unlike the situation in which unions in the corporate and industrial sector find themselves. There we find a dialectical relationship between unions on the one hand, and management representing shareholders on the other. When one side takes a stance on some or another issue, it will be confronted by the other force and a genuine dialectic exists that provides at least some possibility of balanced judgment in the result.

In the case of the educational unions, by contrast and by and large, the normal dialectical relationships do not exist because the structures that are alleged to rule over union activity are structures that have been, for the most part, co-opted by the professional educational unions, bureaucratic structures, and the like. The school boards simply do not function as normal controls on unions, and, as a result, you have particularly powerful union organizations within the public school arena. At a more general level, we should note that the public sector unions have been the only sources of union growth in recent years precisely because they do not have a normal dialectical relationship, and tend to reflect monopolistic service sectors. But least of all do the educational unions exist in a controlled environment. They exist in an often essentially uncontrolled environment for the reasons that I have here given.

In addition to the unions representing public school personnel, typically within states there are regional and state-level bureaucratic structures that also work to reinforce the status quo. In the case of Wisconsin, for example, the Department of Public Instruction now being dismantled and replaced by a Department of Education, has traditionally been a near-perfect representation of EFM, attempting to block at every turn any effort to permit parents to decide how education dollars should be allocated.

In most states, whether called the Department of Public Instruction or the Department of Education, the structures in question have become, over the years, essentially operatives in favor of the maintenance of the educational finance monopoly. In addition to state and regional activities there are, of course, very powerful national unions doing essentially the same thing. The National Educational Association and the American Federation of Teachers are the prominent and dominant national organizations, always ready to jump into local frays and to assist their local chapters and organizations.

For example, in noted cases such as California in the case of the pro-school choice Proposition 174 in 1993, essential opposition came both from the professional organizations at the state levels, such as the California Teachers Association, but also their national organizations, the NEA and AFT. They wanted to make certain, by providing money, counsel, personnel support, professional direction, and so on, that Proposition 174 not only lost at the ballot, but lost ingloriously, enshrouded in the most acrid smoke screens, essentially scandalous accusations that came forth from the organizations opposing it. In chapter 11 we will examine more closely the specifically political structures and strategies on which EFM's defenders of the status quo have relied. It will be useful at this juncture to make evident what exactly I mean when I accuse such groups of working to sustain the status quo. Very often these defenders of EFM ask, heatedly, "How *dare* you call us defenders of the status quo. Do you not know that we are constantly seeking reform of American K-12 education in all jurisdictions? Given that constant promotion of reform, how can anyone accuse us of defending the status quo?"

As usual, the key to solving the only-apparent puzzle presented by these contradictory positions lies in the definition of terms. It is certainly true, indeed obviously true, that among the defenders of contemporary American education and of EFM there is something like a dedication to perpetual, even permanent, reform. This is what is often called "King for a Day" reform mentality. Reform after reform after reform come pouring out of the word processors of the educational establishment, each such reform constituting a witness to the failure of those that preceded it. So, yes, it is certainly true that EFM's defenders are seeking reform, seeking change, and in that sense are not wedded to the status quo.

But, of course, that is not what I and others like me are talking about when we call such folk captives of the status quo and defenders thereof.

What I am referring to when I make such allegations is the incontrovertible fact that these people are absolutely stuck in defense of the status quo when one understands the essence of that status quo as EFM itself, that is, a funding mechanism. "Educational reform"—we hear a great deal about it. We see a lot of activity in its name. It is used to justify expenditure after expenditure, new programs and new personnel, the very proliferation of personnel and program that I often write about. All of this activity and all of this sought-after change carries with it the understanding, however—indeed, has as its first principle—that it must not under any circumstances tamper with the monopolistic assignment of tax dollars dedicated to education. It must not tamper with educational finance monopoly itself.

So, another mystery is solved. The mystery of how we can say EFM's defenders work for the status quo even as they feverishly pursue "reform" is no mystery at all. We are simply not talking about the same thing. EFM is defended by those who love the status quo as defined by the funding mechanism which is the very essence of contemporary K-12 education. That is the status quo defense that I am talking about.

Indeed, embarrassingly, those who cry for perpetual reform of K-12 short of any tampering with educational finance monopoly, if they would but think about it, would recognize that constant reforms, "King for a Day" reforms, are in and of themselves a crucial warning sign that educational finance monopoly must be junked. For in a rational and healthy environment one does not talk about major reform as a constant. One *reforms* for a *purpose*, as a means works for the end. Constant reform is a sign of organizational sickness, disorientation, and loss of purpose. Any dynamic policy and the social structures created by that policy will always be evolving, of course, changing in tune with circumstances, applying principles to those new circumstances and manifesting novelty in those applications. But if we are constantly reforming in fundamental senses, it means we have lost our way, gotten off the track. As regards American K-12 education, we are in the throes of constant, perpetual, even permanent reform *within* the system. We are disoriented. And educational finance monopoly is the malady which makes all such reforms unsatisfying and insufficient. That is the status quo EFM's defenders cling to, the status quo which needs to be dismantled in favor of parental freedom through school choice without financial penalty.

The desperate and sudden complete reversal, to push for public-school-only choice as a diversionary tactic of the California Teachers Association (CTA) during the Proposition 174 battle, for example, is an excellent illustration of the lengths to which the vested interests will go in order to maintain the status quo, understood to be a funding mechanism ("School Voucher Threat Gives Impetus for Reform," *Los Angeles Times*, November 11, 1993). The Milwaukee Teachers' Education Association (MTEA) offers another good example of a teachers' union suddenly "converting" to choice (i.e., public-school-only choice) as exemplified by a symposium held on "Public School Reform" in May of 1994, which included an "MTEA Initiative for School Reform Within Milwaukee Public Schools." The initiative supported open enrollments, charter school proposals, and the like, all aimed at diverting attention away from genuine school choice. It was obvious that the unions were running scared. (See, e.g., "Reality Check: MTEA Tries to Head Off School Reform From Outside," *Milwaukee Sentinel*, May 13, 1994; "Teachers' Union Hopes Vote Shows They Support School Reform, Too," *Milwaukee Journal*, May 12, 1994; "MTEA Acts to Head Off Privatization," *Milwaukee Sentinel*, May 12, 1994) When on one day they are strongly opposing public school choice, and on the next day they are actively endorsing it, it seems evident that this switch was just a superficial conversion of convenience, provoked by the realization that it could be a useful way to fend off genuine choice. Such behavior is neither surprising nor especially shameful. But those of us who know that parents, all schools, and all children will benefit from school choice without financial penalty should not be taken in by it, nor hesitate to point to the inadequacy of such measures.

Looked at from a different perspective, one can ask whether EFM's core defenders, in opposing school choice so vehemently, may in truth be flying in the face of their own particular interests. Even if school choice means the loss of monopolistic and self-perpetuating controls over educational funding—and it does—that may be a much better fate than the ultimate collapse of the system in the face of social and political despair and abandonment of the educational status quo. Puerto Rico's pioneering but ill-fated limited school choice program in its first two years obviously helped San Juan's public schools and new community schools take on new vitality, even as it provided hope and help to all parents and, indirectly, many private schools. Odd Eiken, the Minister for Schools, described in the November 29, 1993, London *Times* exactly the same effect flowing from Sweden's new choice provisions. Contrast such realities with, for example, Hartford, Connecticut's, desperation over the condition of its public schools and consequent choice of a private contractor to run its schools. Did EFM's defenders choose wisely? Might support or tolerance of school choice have been a wiser path, even from a self-interest perspective?

Such a case can be made quite powerfully. However, finally, that is more an interesting side question than it is the essence of things. The ultimate question of educational funding is not how comfortably we provide for EFM's defenders, but how well we provide justice to parents and children, justice in the form of family support and educational integrity and quality.

In addition to the directly involved and directly financially dependent groups such as I have here described, EFM also derives great support from groups that have what amount to interlocking directorates with the core EFM defenders, the materially benefitting defenders such as those described above.

Perhaps the most important of these relationships is in the local, state, and national Parent-Teacher Associations (PTAs). The very idea of organizations devoted to promoting interaction between parents and teachers seems positive, warm, good. There is a problem in the reality of things, however. The problem is that the "parent" aspect of "PTA" has become essentially the handmaid of the professional, unionized "teacher" dimension of the term.

What this means, at its core, is this: the PTAs, instead of providing balance and critical perspective on the workings of the monopoly's schools and staff, have been converted into tools. Because of their massive number—current PTA membership is more than 7,000,000, it reports—and the positive, apple pie image the very name conveys, parents who identify with PTAs can be a substantial political force. Being essentially subservient to the educational professionals who constitute the rest of the PTA membership, and following closely the political agenda established by the educator's unions, the NEA and the AFT, the result is simple and devastating to the parents' own interests. For example, and of special interest for our purposes, PTAs across the land, slavishly following the lead of the NEA and AFT, uniformly oppose true school choice which, as we have seen, consists entirely of advancing *parents'* prerogatives. This is as classic an example as we will find of parents' captivity. The parents in the PTAs have, in effect, been taken prisoner by their professional educational "partners." The prison doors are unlocked, we know, but PTA parents have yet to learn that they should arise and remove their barriers. (A very useful examination of these issues can be found in Charlene K. Haar, "PTA Serves Teacher Unions, Not Parents," *Insight on the News*, March 27, 1995.)

There are other interlocking directorates of comparable sort. I think here particularly of the incidence of NAACP interconnections with the educational unions, and also the educational union participation in the Democratic party. The latter will be treated much more extensively in chapter 11, where we look at the political triangles established to maintain educational finance monopoly. But the interconnection between the NAACP and similar groups, on the one hand; and the local and national educational unions, on the other; goes a long way to explain the seemingly paradoxical fact: minority parents overwhelmingly support school choice, while their "community leaders" overwhelmingly oppose it. No paradox, really. The "leaders" are not representing their constituents on this vital subject, but their own interests in the school funding status quo.

There are other groups that have been supporters of educational finance monopoly as a way to block a different development which they do not want to occur. It is not easy to characterize this, but in general what I am talking about is the incidence of groups which express concern for religious activity in society and see efforts in favor of school choice essentially as an at least religious, probably Christian, and probably Roman Catholic, camel's nose under the tent. These groups imagine that school choice, instead of being the expansion of parental freedom which it is, is in actuality just a subterfuge behind which religious interests are trying to advance their particular causes. Thus, for example, we find certain liberal Jewish organizations typically expressing antipathy for school choice and arguing for the maintenance of the educational status quo, EFM. The Americans United for the Separation of Church and State, (formerly POAU, Protestants & Other Americans United) is a classic illustration of what I am talking about, of course. And to a considerable extent the ACLU's interests at state and national levels in preventing school choice seems also to be motivated by concerns for what they take to be religious intrusion.

We see this, moreover, in much of the press, as illustrated at the *New York Times* and the *Milwaukee Journal Sentinel* for example. Such papers have provided a sustaining opposition to school choice and, when pushed into the corner and forced to define their ultimate interests, they appear to be more concerned with the prevention of what they would take to be religious influence in education than anything else. It is the kind of thing which has driven such traditional Democrats as Milwaukee Mayor John Norquist, for example, surveying the mayhem in many public schools, to say that the problem of American urban education is "not Bibles, but bullets." This is a graphic and dramatic illustration of the frustration that school choice advocates feel when they encounter the drum beat of misguided religious concern from such sources as the *New York Times*, *Milwaukee Journal Sentinel* and other papers that ape them.

The ultimate reason that such people have for opposing school choice does indeed seems to be about religion. "Violation of church and state separation" is always their last refuge. But in occupying this position they betray a radical failure to understand the essential nature of freedom in contemporary democracies, including the United States. They are reflecting, instead, a seventeenth- or eighteenth-century mentality, imagining papal or some other capacity to intrude and manipulate the workings of government. That is not how religion enters into the public order in the democratic age. To the extent religion can exercise a vital role in modern circumstances, it can do it only through the hearts and minds of believers-as-citizens. Those citizens may derive some of their politically pertinent values from their religious beliefs, and seek their manifestation in appropriate ways in society's values and policies. They will be successful precisely insofar as they can find enough other citizens to share, not their *religious* creed, but their *political* values. Politics, always about the business of assigning values, will draw them from any source. Religion may well be one of them. But those values will enter as *political* values manifested by citizens—and to attempt to invalidate them *a priori*, because they may be religiously rooted, is simply to imagine that we are in an age of Inquisition in which religiously motivated citizens are actually "agents of the Pope." The other drastic error in the charge that school choice is a religious ruse is, in many respects, even more egregious. It fails entirely to grasp a fundamental truth noted repeatedly in this volume. There are *many* motives which bring people to school choice advocacy, many constituencies. Religious motive is but one, and can never be successful without becoming part of a larger political coalition—and that, again, belies the charge of "church and state" violation.

And then we have a second group of people that I refer to as the "altruistic corollaries" of EFM's defense and defenders. These are the people who have no direct material benefit flowing from educational finance monopoly but who have been somehow convinced over time that the welfare of "the kids," as they say, and perhaps of society itself, is somehow bound up with EFM's maintenance. And thus, for example, the *parent* components of PTAs, the parents who obviously do not have a material benefit flowing from EFM, the parents who associate with the PTAs, nonetheless become operatives supporting educational finance monopoly and they do so because they are secure in the knowledge that they are "doing a good thing" when they work with the school systems represented by the PTAs.

Similarly, the thousands of school boards around the country tend to be populated by people whose essential motive seems to be good will for all. They certainly do not normally have destructive motives. They certainly would not consciously desire to maintain a humanly destructive policy, such as educational finance monopoly. Nonetheless, once they begin serving in the school board capacity, surrounded as they are by the professionals, they tend to be co-opted for purposes of maintenance of the funding status quo and become defenders thereof.

Similar developments have occurred with traditional civic and community leadership, whether in fraternal or business organizations. They have traditionally been mesmerized by the system they begin to work with. Essentially what such people fall prey to is the emotional conviction that tells them they are doing something good when they are working for schools; and, after all, most of the kids are in the public schools; therefore, if we work with the public schools we are doing something good. Through such altruistic but uncritical processes, a desire to "help the kids" by offering their support to *education* becomes transformed into "let's help the public schools." And at that point, instead of becoming people and agencies able to say "Let us concentrate on education and ask of all alternative delivery systems how good a job they are doing" they have become victims of the classic ends-means confusion. What has happened to them is that through a kind of mesmerization, under the influence of the sense of doing something good, they have become agents of the status quo rather than evaluators thereof. Very often, this has happened because otherwise capable people, concerned for failing educational conditions, have made the wrong diagnosis, imagined the wrong cure, and turned to the wrong experts. Too often, parents and citizens imagine, because they have been led to imagine, that the essential educational contest is over how to do education, for example, what pedagogical approaches or curriculum reform, or class size will be best in contemporary society. Were that the reality of things, it would appear to be entirely logical to call upon educators as the most likely sources of expert advice, and to submit to their guidance. After all, when the water pipes spring a leak, we call a plumber. When our sickness is diagnosed as cancer, we call an oncologist.

Unfortunately, to understand the central problems of American education that way is to *misunderstand* them. To treat them on the basis of that misunderstanding is to *mistreat* them. The basic struggle in American education is not about how to do education. The basic struggle is about who will control the assignment of such tax dollars as society wants to spend on education. And the basic options in that struggle are, as we have seen, on the one hand, educational finance monopoly, the status quo in which all tax dollars are assigned by bureaucratic monopolies at state and district levels; and, on the other hand, school choice without financial penalty, in which parents assign some or all of education tax dollars to the public or private schools they think best for their children.

When we see clearly the essential truth that today's battle is really over public policy—how to assign education-dedicated tax dollars, knowing the prices we always pay for monopoly, and the rewards we reap from free decisions—then many other confusions are instantly overcome. For guidance on this crucial public policy question we would not turn rationally to professional educators, for two reasons: first, as such they have no expertise on the public policy issues, as contrasted with what we hope is their expertise on pedagogical matters; second, insofar as they are members of unions and bureaucratic structures whose material welfare is directly tied to finance monopoly, they are just an interest group like any other special interests rather than disinterested experts.

We can understand clearly, too, certain other things which, unless we see the essentially political and monetary nature of today's conflict, seem extremely paradoxical. For example, this insight explains why urban public school teachers and staff, financially able even though typically not wealthy, choose to send their children to private schools at greatly higher rates than citizens generally—even as they vigorously oppose a policy of school choice for parents with fewer funds available. (See, e.g., Denis P. Doyle, "Lessons in Hypocrisy," *Wall Street Journal*, June 13 1995.) The educators choose the private schools disproportionately because they esteem them and contemn their own public schools disproportionately. But at the same time they fight against choice for all because they judge that their material interests—the very finances which enable them to choose—depend on maintaining the finance monopoly. No genuine paradox here.

Another only-apparent paradox is also solved by seeing the basically financial and political nature of today's struggle. Why up to now have America's citizens and parents routinely and overwhelmingly expressed support for school choice in the abstract, and then turned around and opposed it in the concrete, as in California, November, 1993? In part, that is because the attractive essence of school choice has sometimes been blurred in the specific proposal made. Thus, for example, California's Proposition 174 had various unnecessary impediments in it. But, even more important, the educator-defenders of EFM, the monopolistic status quo, have managed to convince huge elements of the media, the citizenry, the PTAs, and state legislators, that the issue is educational, having to do with the educational welfare of "the kids" (rather than the material welfare of the educators). If that were true, then responsible citizens and parents understandably might be expected to turn to the educationalist "experts" for counsel. And when they listen to those experts, what do they hear? They hear that, as the California Teachers Association said, school choice—that is, parental freedom to decide where their children will go to school—is so *evil* that citizens should not even have a chance to consider it! ("The 'Evil' in California," *Wall Street Journal*, September 14, 1992).

Scary stuff, indeed. The only problem with it is this: it is a radical untruth, spoken by sources entirely unable to evaluate the issue not because they are evil or corrupt, but because they are entirely wedded to the status quo and its material benefits. The unadorned facts are that school choice can only improve the educational effort, in both public and private schools; encourage parent control and involvement; introduce the possibility of rational and responsive educational budgeting; and forever rid us of the program and personnel proliferation, bureaucratic mushrooming, and self-servingness characteristic of monopolistic structures.

It is simply senseless to turn to monopoly-protected educators for "expert" advice on whether the monopoly should be replaced by parents allocating tax dollars assigned to education. One does not ask the fox how to secure the hen house. The sickness is not the cure. The cure will come when citizens and community and political leaders blow away the smoke of a false "expertise" and exercise their own good judgment: educational finance monopoly is harmful to our health, but school choice without financial penalty is good for what ails us.

Lacking a material dependency on EFM, civic organizations and business structures that have so often succumbed to its allure are finally open to the truth if it is presented to them seriously. Once they see the light, they can be powerful forces for expanding parental freedom and ending finance monopoly. The recent, trailblazing enactment of limited but true school choice in Milwaukee (July, 1995) owed much to the Metropolitan Milwaukee Association of Commerce (MMAC), for instance. MMAC had long devoted much of its civic energy to "the schools," with the usual frustrating results. In 1991, MMAC leadership began looking hard at the "mesmerization" issue, and began to probe alternative ways of conceptualizing the education problem and their response thereto. An extended process of discussion and analysis led to a crucial breakthrough in 1993: MMAC, breaking out of the ends-means trap, declared that parental empowerment *via* school choice was their top educational objective. And, not long after, money went where mouth was, personnel were hired, and organizing activities began that contributed substantially to the ultimate achievement of true school choice in Wisconsin. This and other cases show clearly that EFM's spell can be broken if organizations will bring to education the same critical thinking they bring to other areas of endeavor. Even more important, it is vital to note that there routinely is, among the population broadly, great support for school choice when people are asked intelligent and objectively correct questions as to whether or not parents deserve wider influence in the choice of educational environments for their children. The September, 1992, results of a national Gallup Poll sponsored by the National Catholic Educational Association are representative: When asked if they would support using tax money now going to public schools to send children to public, private, or parochial schools, 61 percent of adults surveyed said they would, while 38 percent said they would not. Seventy percent expressed general support for a voucher system in which parents would receive government funding for education, while only 27 percent opposed vouchers.

An even more interesting illustration of the fact that, with all its efforts, with all its inertia and supporting personnel and rhetorical smoke, EFM has finally not been convincing, can be seen in the results of a famous exit poll done among California voters as they left Proposition 174 polling places, November 2 , 1993. Even as they were thumping the *specific*, viciously maligned, school choice effort in Proposition 174 by a 70-30 margin, they were *affirming* their support for the concept of school choice and parental freedom by an even wider margin. (Luntz Weber California Exit Poll, Luntz Weber Research and Strategic Services, November 3, 1993.)

So as better to understand such gaping discrepancies, it will be very useful to examine more concentratedly the arsenal of smoke screens employed to block such specific efforts as Proposition 174. There has been in all such cases an incessant series of pseudo-arguments, which have kept many objective critics off the scent of true reform. The next chapter will analyze some of the most prominent and effective of these diversions, and will show their inadequacy if truth be our guide.

10

Why Are We in a Quagmire?
III: The Rhetorical Tools of EFM's Defenders

In the chapters preceding this one, I have on several occasions referred to various of the smoke screens used by educational finance monopoly defenders to help in its defense. In this chapter I want to go more deeply into why I have employed such a pejorative expression to characterize the rhetorical defenses of EFM supporters. Since "smoke screens" *is* pejorative, might not I myself be using it as a smoke screen? That is a legitimate concern.

I have spent the last four decades completely devoted to and involved in the world of intellectual exchange. Not only have I lived and worked in that world, but for many years at Marquette University I had much responsibility for ensuring conditions in which the free flow of ideas could occur and was encouraged. From such a life one develops habits of looking at all sides, of being open to correction through dialectical processes, and of realizing that even a poorly presented position may have significant truth attaching to it. Truly seen, the life of intellect, unlike, for example, that of a debate contestant or a trial attorney, does not have "victory" as its goal, but, rather, the optimum grasp of the truth of things.

I mention this to make clear that I did not arrive lightly at the conclusion that EFM's primary defenders rely on smoke rather than seriously grounded argument. My normal instinct would be, and should be, to engage such people with the expectation of learning from them, as well as the hope of helping them to see whatever part of the truth is in my possession. That normal instinct would be badly followed in this instance, however. The rhetorical defenses of EFM are not well-honed survivors of intellectual exchange. They are simply tools designed to achieve "victory," and victory means keeping in place the monopolistic policies from which material benefits derive.

115

In the great British naval movies, if a British ship ran out of ammunition, or lost use of its guns, the command would come down: "Make smoke!" If one wants to defend a position, but one's reasons are such that, while perfectly understandable, they do not have the objective power to convince others, what are the temptations that present themselves? The temptations are smoke screens, red herrings, non sequiturs. In other words, the temptation is to move away from central preoccupation with the truth of things, and in the direction of finding those things that will defend one's position, not intellectually or analytically but effectively in the rhetorical or political worlds. When someone succumbs to such temptations we certainly would not describe that kind of activity as heroic. We would not even describe it as virtuous. But we need not describe it as vicious, either. It is most assuredly not unusual. People like to win, and they like to butter their bread. And many folks much of the time honor many things before they honor the truth. For these purposes it is important to distinguish between truthfulness, on the one hand, and honesty, on the other. A dedication to truthfulness means far more than simply being honest by inclination. Dedication to truthfulness means being a slave to the truth, willing to suffer for it, dedicated to it in a definitive and final sense. Being honest simply means that you do not intend to tell lies. And that distinction is extremely important if we are to understand but not demonize the defenders of educational finance monopoly. Being a slave to the truth is different from not being a liar.

An important point pertinent to this case, as noted earlier, is that most observers are disposed to take "educators" more at face value than they would other social groups. The presumption appears to be that educators, being educators, are in some sense more altruistic and less self-interested, perhaps, than are other groups within society. Educators are, after all, dedicated to "the kids," are in the "nonprofit sector," and so on. This habit of taking educators at face value is not a very good idea when we are talking about issues in which self-interest is involved. When it comes to one's own self-interest, the distinction between profit-seeking and nonprofit seeking is eliminated for all practical purposes.

To illustrate the point, let us consider briefly a February 27, 1995, letter from the president of the Jersey City Education Association, Inc. (the local teachers' union) to a probationary teacher who had not paid his or her union dues. The terms and categories of the letter have *nothing* to do with education, and *everything* to do with the material benefits flowing from the monopoly contracts they have been able to forge on the basis of union solidarity. Such solidarity "is one of the main reasons that our contract ranks with the best in the nation. You have already received the benefits of our last negotiations. The starting salary was increased from $25,610 to $32,000 and the maximum from $51,030 to $61,800.... The BA maximum is the highest in the state, if not in the country. In addition you now have free family prescriptions and family optical. You also have a tuition reimbursement plan and your M.A. and M.A. & 32 levels have been increased from $1,500 to $2,400." And so on it goes, entirely devoted to such provisions, and with no reference to the horrendous educational results in Jersey City which have driven mayor and governor and education commissioner to the conviction that the monopoly must be broken and school choice provided to Jersey City parents.

The attitudes expressed in the letter reflect a definitive logical disconnection between ends and means, and simply portray the inclination of a group with monopoly protection to serve itself rather than the objective needs for which it exists. And it shows well enough the contextual point of this chapter: educational unions serve the same material welfare as do unions generally, and that is perfectly acceptable and understandable. But it also means that their rhetorical defenses should be submitted to the same critical analysis as any other seeker after material benefits.

Similarly, and again related to an issue discussed above, the normal adversarial control mechanisms in the employment structures of education are missing. The school boards that one might think of as being the control mechanisms, tend in fact to be co-opted by the professional educators so that the line employed by union and bureaucratic structures tends to become the school board's line, and also the line of civic community organizations. And that means that when the citizens and politicians hear that line it seems as if they are hearing the outcome of a broad-based social dialogue that produced consensus, when in fact they are typically just hearing from organizations that have been voluntarily but unwittingly co-opted by self-interested parties such as the bureaucratic and educational union structures. The normal clarifying dialectic that one expects from social interchange and counterbalances tends not to occur in the educational arena. Smoke screens will not be a surprising or shocking development in such an environment, and we will examine some of the more prominent ones.

Educational Choice as "Experimental"

Chapter 6 constitutes a thoroughgoing refutation of this classic smoke screen befogging the issue of parental choice vs. monopoly. Such choice, provided by unrestricted educational vouchers, for example, is often portrayed as essentially experimental. As such, its allegedly unknown results can be described as risky, and the argument made that prudent people do not trade in a known system, even if it has severe problems, for an unknown one. Therefore, in this view, one cannot propose unrestricted choice programs until, by an unspecified amount of experimentation, we have "proved" its efficacy and harmlessness. Then, if we insist on very difficult and restrictive terms for the experiments and difficult if not impossible standards for assessment, we have made "proving" unlikely and thus foredoomed unrestricted choice, without ever condemning it absolutely.

That is clever smoke, and it is not surprising that even some friends of choice get blinded by it. We all want to be cautious, do we not? Cautious, yes. Bamboozled, no! The legitimacy and superiority of educational outcomes when choice is operating are not experimental but well known, as chapter 6 makes evident. While chapter 6 dwells especially on the happy experiences of other democracies with school choice, here I just want to call attention particularly and once again to America's own premier true school choice history: America's Catholic schools. At elementary and secondary levels, the tremendous contributions of the Catholic religious orders made it possible to erect the Catholic school system by "choice," because those contributions in effect offset the financial penalty for so doing. As the orders and their contributions dwindled, educational costs escalated, and finance monopoly caused all tax dollars to flow to public schools, the relative presence of that Catholic system in American education inevitably shrank. But even in its present embattled state it remains the envy of educators everywhere.

What can be said of that Catholic reality can similarly be said of all the other private school systems, religious or not, elementary, secondary, and higher, in this country. In terms of educational outcomes they represent much of the best in American education and, in every case, reflect the salutary results of educational choices made. They represent educational choice against the tides created by public-financing monopolies. One can only imagine how much their fruitful experiences would have been magnified if true choice, without severe financial penalty, existed in the United

States. Be that as it may, we already know this: study after study, the directly pertinent experiences of other nations, and the too-rarely noted but vast history of American educational choice in operation all show that choice *works*, and cannot rationally be described as "experimental."

Avoiding the Trap of Confusing Evidence and Analysis: Automatic Results of Educational Choice

One specific aspect of the "experiment" trap that deserves comment is that choice's superiority is not dependent on quantification and measurement through comparative test scores and graduation rates. Choice passes all such tests with flying colors, but many of the qualitative dimensions of choice's excellence are also worth noting. Indeed, as I see it, some of school choice's best friends have been too eager to think they could "prove" what needs not statistical validation but logical analysis. When such statistical proofs are not forthcoming, thus, those who judge them imperative say "no proof of choice's superiority has been offered." Yes, it has been *definitively* offered, as logical analysis makes plain. Thus, for example, we note that the simple act of adopting a voucher-type system would break forever the monopoly-encouraging system now existing, kill the self-serving characteristics of such a system, and enable parents to fulfill their desire and responsibility to see to their children's education. Were there *no* discernible change in educational outcomes, these would be important accomplishments in social justice, in enhancing family responsibility, and in erasing monopolistic pressure. In the face of them, choice opponents would be obliged to prove that school choice somehow actually *harms* educational attainment, a claim none of them make.

The schools would also be able to establish clear, concrete, and rigorous ethical standards for behavior and instruction, as we saw above. Such standards cannot be implemented in the monopoly-derived public schools in today's circumstances, for those schools, obliged to represent everything, can in fact represent very little in our highly contentious, driven, and litigious society. Serious ethical performance requires specific ethical norms and starting points. Instead, today's public schools inevitably reflect lowest-common-denominator moral postures. Beyond the most rudimentary civic virtues, the moral presentation of state-monopoly schools is confined to "everybody's doing it" secular nostrums—thus, for example, dispensing contraceptives, though that clearly routinizes and thereby legitimizes conduct deemed illicit by many parents—while at the same time refusing to permit abstinence programs reflecting religious scruples against premarital sexual relations. This is a direct result of the monopoly system.

Yet another vitally important good which would stem immediately from educational choice would be the opportunity to control educational costs which today escalate seemingly without relation to performance. The self-serving inclinations of a monopolistic environment—to multiply bureaucracy, to add more and more programs further and further removed from education's essentials, to use poor performance, even failure, as a justification for more funding—would all be attacked instantly by the comparative and competitive environment choice creates. In today's situation, not only do the monopoly-maintained schools face no competition from other schools, but when, as is often the case, those monopolies have independent taxing authority they do not even have to compete with other tax-funded agencies. Educational choice would throw out that corrupting environment, and replace it with one in which anyone qualifying for public funds, whether via parents or public school districts, would be in a comparative and competitive framework enabling taxpayers to ask and clearly answer this question: who is getting the most bang with our bucks? Suddenly, the whole educational enterprise, including the still-vital but no longer monopolistic public systems, would be operating in a responsible atmosphere in which serious evaluation of cost-effectiveness could occur.

All these dynamics would automatically accompany educational choice, do not need demonstration, and further defy the contention that choice is experimental.

Using the Imaginary Perfect to Kill the Practical Good

University of California-Berkeley law professor John Coons is a long-time, deeply committed worker for parental freedom via school choice. When such a person says he cannot support a specific school choice effort such as California's 1993 Proposition #174, because in his judgment it falls *woefully* short of perfection, we can take his action at face value. One may agree or disagree with his particular judgment and prudential analysis, but never doubt the truth of his description of why he acted so, for his dedication to school choice is obvious.

But when staunch defenders of educational finance monopoly, and opponents of parental freedom, use a perfect vision of a perfect school choice abstraction to attack and kill any real-world school choice effort, we would be naive in the extreme if we did not acknowledge the eye-watering smell of serious smoke. This invocation of utopian perfection to obstruct the always-imperfect concrete school choice efforts—always-imperfect, because forced to proceed by partial steps so as not to foul more an already-fouled status-quo—may well be the most common smoke screen. It takes many forms, but a few illustrations will make clear its essential nature.

On July 7, 1995, the House of Representatives Committee on Economic and Educational Opportunities held hearings on a school choice pilot program sponsored by Congressman Riggs of California and Congressman Weldon of Florida. The hearings were broadcast on C-Span Two. One of the persons offering commentary was the president of a national organization of public school administrators. That group is against school choice, not surprisingly. This testimony attacking the pilot program was a classic case of using a perfect to critique a good, knowing the perfect cannot be. Thus: will the pilot programs offer in effect perfect solutions to transportation issues, so parents have *true* choice? Will all special education problems be perfectly met? Will dollars available be sufficient to permit poor parents to purchase *any* private education, no matter how expensive? Will family problems be fixed so that a truly level playing field is achieved by all?

These questions, seen in a realistic context wherein *current* school funding has resulted in the most severe social dislocations, neighborhood abandonments, and parental incapacity to shape children's educational environment, are pure obstructionist efforts. If we were in the state of nature previously described, an enlightened public policy would not only provide for parental freedom but also for any transportation, special education, or family counseling programs it saw fit. But precisely because we are in a morass, and want to be careful not to worsen it as we leave it for school choice, all beginning school choice efforts will be partial, by definition imperfect, and thus subject to critique by comparison with abstract perfections. But such critique is essentially useless, and highly suspect when it comes from those who want above all to maintain EFM.

Church and State

Opponents of choice also suggest that unrestricted parental choice in education would violate constitutional proscriptions against establishing a religion. That was always an illusory interpretation, of course, for parental desire to offer their children an educational environment reflecting their most profound values is simply an admirable extension of parental responsibility, and has nothing to do with the state's establishment of a religion. The previously-mentioned G.I. Bill, riding the crest of patriotic support, should have cleared away the church-state bogeyman, but it did not. Nonetheless, as acknowledged even by lawyers such as Harvard's Lawrence Tribe, not known for "right wing" sympathy, parental vouchers today can pass constitutional muster given the Supreme Court's *Witters, Mueller,* and *Zobrest* precedents of the last decade. Parental freedom was never an actual threat to church-state separation, and now even the artificial constitutional barriers to choice have been lowered. What remains to be done is to blast the church-state specter out of the rhetorical water so that it and other relics of America's public school fixation are no longer used to block parental freedom in education.

Such a definitive demolition of the church-state smoke screen could occur as a result of the litigation now underway on the 1995 expansion of the Milwaukee Parental Choice Program (MPCP) to include religious schools. That expansion made a true choice enterprise, and its September, 1995, start date would make it the first in operation on the mainland. To no one's surprise, the state and national ACLU offices have brought suit against it. Given their resolute stances against religious expression in the public order, they probably had no choice. But those of us dedicated to parental freedom are delighted to have MPCP as the test case, believing, as we do, that it fully meets the criteria of ruling legal precedents, and that, as a result, it can once and for all put to rest the contention that parent-assigned tax dollars constitute undue entanglement of church and state.

Breaking the Bank?

One of the common defenses against educational choice is to charge that it will add to already too-heavy school costs. The position goes along these lines: X is already spent for public schools. Add whatever are the costs of a voucher-type system (Y) and suddenly we have taxes responsible not just for X but X plus Y. That is a neat, but a false, equation. The amount of tax dollars supporting education will be set by public policy. Adding parental choice in and of itself need neither increase nor decrease costs. Rather, what it *necessarily* will do, as noted above, is make possible evaluation of educational outcomes and thus, for the first time, provide a rational basis for allocating and restraining educational money.

A newly adopted voucher system could cost more if, for example, a jurisdiction maintained all current and future public school costs and simply added a voucher system which would help parents of children already in independent schools. But that is an unrealistic scenario. A voucher system designed to hold costs or even roll them back would be a more natural starting method. In such a situation vouchers might begin at a fraction of current public school costs, as illustrated in chapter 7. Even at a fraction, they would encourage some public school parents to send children to independent schools which would reduce the formula-based funding sent to the public schools, and this could easily *reduce* the net tax burden. Over time, a well-designed voucher system would provide the same amount of tax support to parents no matter what public or private schools they chose, but by that time the natural competitive-comparative dynamics of choice can be expected to have overall cost under control at last. Cost savings would accompany dismantling the overgrown bureaucracies and programs characteristic of today's monopoly-protected schools.

"King for a Day"

Another pseudo-argument that has worked against adoption of a parental choice system is the effort to describe it as just one among many educational reforms. Since it is more threatening to deeply entrenched interests, why do we not try all the others before getting serious about choice? Let us set up the list of twenty (or fifteen, or thirty) most popular reform possibilities—school-based management, extended school years, mentoring systems, curricular reforms, even public school-only choice if we are driven to it—and describe unrestricted choice as just one of this large, undetermined number of reform proposals. With any luck, it will get lost and, in any case, unlike the others, it will generate rigorous opposition from vested interests and this should serve to keep it at bay. It is, after all, as even some of its friends are moved to say, "no panacea."

To which John Chubb and Terry Moe and others have responded: "Yes, educational choice *is* a panacea." What they mean is that it is unlike all other educational reforms in the crucial sense that it alone directly attacks the systemic root of so many of today's educational ills: monopoly financing. As we saw earlier, the simple enactment of choice would set in train a variety of positive changes inherent in the system, such as enhanced parental control, responsible environment for educational evaluation, and so on. Equally simply and immediately, it would discourage the program proliferation and bureaucratization characteristic of the bloated public systems resulting from today's finance monopoly. And, even as it naturally and automatically did these things, it would be open to—indeed, encourage—any and all other educational reform initiatives which are before the house. It would encourage them because, in the now-freed atmosphere created by choice, there is every reason to imagine that careful educational experimentation would flourish.

Parental choice in education is reform of the system itself, it is unlike all other reforms, and, given the severity of the problems stemming from today's educational systems, it is about as close to a true panacea as we are likely to come in this life.

Fear of Freedom

But freedom is a terrible and dangerous thing! Just look at David Duke and one can see the extremism that exists in America, and then imagine that extremism locating itself in American education via the freedom provided by choice! Or, what about the California "witches" who announced that, if Proposition #174 were passed, they would immediately establish a school? That is a scary picture, indeed. It is entirely a fabrication, but a spooky one. Its unreality lies in the fact that, under a choice program a political jurisdiction can establish whatever antiextremism rules it chooses to adopt, including provisions against racism, sexism, or any other "ism" judged intolerable by legitimate authority. Any group unwilling to abide by such rules simply would not be permitted to participate in the program. Independent schools already exist within a network of governing regulations and voluntary associational rules which means, among other things, that the vision of "extremism" is just a classic scare tactic.

But, "He Who Pays the Piper..."

There is yet another smoke screen which is a bit more subtle and which, in any case, is more important. Its importance derives from the fact that it is used both by classic EFM defenders and, in essentially identical language, by persons often described, and accurately described, as libertarian, on the "far right wing." Because it has shown the ability to attract such widely divergent groups to its use, we will look at length at this particular misportrayal of the truth of things.

Most of our favorite slogans contain real truth, no doubt. But, as is the way with slogans, they are often stated with an absoluteness belied by the facts. "You get what you pay for" comes to mind. The next time that common expression is heard, the reader might ask why, then, we also hear of consumer fraud, shysterism, and the advantages of comparison shopping—each of which establishes clearly that you do not necessarily "get what you pay for." There is truth in the slogan, but stated absolutely it is much more a hope than a reality.

Another slogan often proclaimed with unwarranted absoluteness, and one heard often in school choice discussions, is "He who pays the piper calls the tune." There are those who ask: "If tax dollars become available to buy private education, must not private education be corrupted thereby, perhaps even so corrupted as to vitiate entirely the reason for breaking the current educational finance monopoly? Might those tax dollars simply convert the independent schools into quasi-public ones, finally killing off what is left of the private sector?" Such inquiries are often followed by "After all, he who pays..."

This is a particularly interesting concern because, ironically enough, it is expressed with equal vigor by two radically different sorts of people. It is expressed by some who think of themselves as libertarians, and it is expressed by some who might accurately be described as statists, persons very accommodating of increased governmental activity generally.

The statists want to counsel against vouchers no doubt for many reasons, but one they often give is that even student-carried aid should and would make the recipient schools part of the state network, and thus subservient, for example, to a state Department of Public Instruction, and thus finally indistinguishable from public schools. Therefore, "for their own sake," it is said, private schools and their proponents should not ask for voucher-type systems. One may wonder about the sincerity of such a position when it is announced by leaders of educational unions, the National Educational Association, and groups of that sort. For them, it could be simply a convenient scare tactic and smoke screen used to maintain their finance monopoly.

Be that as it may, the argument is much like, indeed essentially identical to, that of the libertarian-type who says, "He who pays the piper calls the tune." That person believes that any tax dollars, no matter the distribution method, will ultimately and inevitably become a vehicle for state dominance and loss of independent identity. Believing that, it is not surprising he reaches the same conclusion as the statist: private schools and their proponents should not ask for voucher-type programs.

To both statist and concerned libertarian I respond as follows: in reaching your conclusion, you have managed to collapse and obliterate several crucial logical distinctions which, if restored, will collapse and obliterate your conclusion. Restored, they will make clear that we can find ways to break finance monopoly, install parents as decision-makers regarding finance distribution, *and* avoid state dominance.

As context, we must recall the severity of the present situation. The symptoms of current American education difficulties are devastating. The negative results ramify outward in many directions. The independent sector is under great pressure, and the forces of educational finance monopoly (EFM) are expanding their tentacles, and deepening their roots. We are not talking about a small or slow problem that prudently might never justify sharp departure from past practice. We are rather talking about a profound and seductive problem that may well justify a dramatic departure and some degree of risk. To avoid it simply because there is some risk involved would be a bit like not throwing a rope to a drowning person for fear that that person *may* get blisters from clutching the rope as he is pulled to safety, the blisters *may* become infected, and the infection *may* become life-threatening. That displays a fundamental lack of proportion in assessing degrees of risk and immediate *vs* remote dangers. We can, indeed, must, work to save American education, even if we recognize a bit of risk in doing so.

But not much risk, I think. Let us start by making certain key distinctions without which we and reason are lost. Let us distinguish between ownership and assistance; between sponsorship and support; between managing operations and assessing outcomes; and between tendencies and laws.

The first three distinctions invite us to see palpable differences on vital questions of control, definition, and essential character. The words and the ideas they represent express different realities in any common sense usage. Can they be abused? Can real differences be eroded? Can offered support become *de facto* sponsorship and control? Of course, if vigilance is not maintained. But that is the point of the fourth distinction, the distinction between tendencies and laws.

While ownership necessarily conveys control, latent or active, assistance of an independent entity need not convey control. I can freely choose to help a person or an agency and forego any control, or even influence over it. If it takes on a character I do not value, I can withdraw my support. If the thing I have supported is craven, or other-directed, it may let my action unduly influence its behavior, or it may take the occasion to reexamine itself and freely redefine. But in none of those eventualities has support become control. Thus the point about paying the piper and calling the tune: they *tend* to go together; they do not *have* to go together.

The distinction between managing operations and judging outcomes brings F.A. Hayek to mind. In *The Road to Serfdom* we find him distinguishing rigorously and crucially between providing rules of the road, on the one hand, and telling people where to go, on the other. We find him distinguishing between "signposts and commanding people which road to take." These are realistic distinctions with special pertinence to educational choice vs. finance monopoly.

If we bring this same rigor to bear on education policy, we will see a road with several forks or junctures, and we will be blind if we do not see the differences between the forks when we encounter them. Let us start at the beginning.

- At the first fork in the road we decide either to accept the need for government or that we are truly anarchists.
- If we decide government is necessary, then we either accept that government can have a legitimate concern for education, for the social and personal welfare of the nation, or we deny it.
- If we accept some governmental concern for education, we will either provide tax dollars for it, or we will provide no tax dollars for it.
- If we provide tax dollars for it, we will stream all those dollars to the governmental schools through vehicles of monopoly financing (Hayek's telling people where to go), or we will disperse those public dollars via parents and their free acts of choice.
- If we choose to disperse, we can exercise in the dispersal great control of and intrusion in educational operations, or we can rely on results assessment, and very little prescription, as our dispersal technique (Hayek's establishing rules of the road, but letting the traveler decide his pathway).

Dispersed spending at the state level would have a happy corollary effect: by diminishing the role of central state authorities, it would lessen federal capacity to intrude via such state agencies.

If one's purpose in dispersing is to break monopoly and expand freedom of choice, then it is not easy to see why anyone would settle for an entangling method. It is analytically evident that a voucher, grant, or tax credit system could be created which would diminish state presence and enhance parental freedom in education.

If despite such logical displays one still believes that these distinctions are only lifeless abstractions that do not touch the central and dominating realities of governmental funding, then let us consider certain very real and lively historical cases. First, let us look at the United States as it is. In fifty states we see a monopoly of educational finance producing humanly destructive results, the very results which have produced the crisis of contemporary American education. This is not a speculative possibility or tendency, but an overwhelming and urgent fact.

Second, we can look at Europe in which many countries have state-owned and supported schools, but within those schools religious variety among them (there being no artificial church-state complications), providing the occasion for choice by parents. Even this is much different from and superior to what prevails in the United States, in my judgment. Third, if we look at Denmark, Sweden, or Australia, for example, we find direct state aid to independent institutions but not ownership, nor sponsorship, nor direction of those schools, which are free creations reflecting religious, cultural, and philosophical motivations and true parental freedom. This naturally encourages greatly variegated educational offerings with excellent educational results. The distinctions I have pointed to among these three existing alternatives are very substantial and undeniably real.

Now, let us look at a fourth alternative. Let us call that the United States-I-hope-for. The accident of alleged church-state entanglements means that the most likely method for achieving parental freedom in the United States is a voucher system or a tax credit program that would not involve any direct tax dollars to schools, but would allow parents to allocate those dollars to the schools they choose for their children, with the dynamic and liberating results noted above. Precedents in our own experience abound. The GI Bill, which had no practical encumbrances, is a powerful precedent. In Wisconsin and in many other states, various tuition grant programs for colleges and universities exist and, again, have essentially no encumbering and complicating character attaching to them. Preschool voucher programs involving independent schools are common and not troublesome. Stepping outside the educational framework for a moment, if we look at the method of social security disbursement in the United States, we see a clear case of governmental dollars with no restrictions as to use. They are simply disbursed in the form of a check—a voucher, in effect. If Mrs. O'Reilly wants to turn that check over to Fr. O'Malley at St. Mary's, no one will try to stop her on church-state grounds. Thus, experience and logic coincide to make clear that the simple presence of tax-derived dollars does not inevitably corrupt. Everything depends on the method of their use.

We can use fire without burning ourselves. We know that using electricity in the United States will result in some unfortunate accidents in any given year. But we are very unlikely to pull the plug on electricity. We know that a system of private property will result in some hedonistic excesses and some personal deprivations, and while we look for ways to refine and limit such unhappy results, we steadfastly defend private property as, on balance, the most humanly fulfilling economic formation.

If we break educational finance monopoly, and replace it with parental freedom, based on tax dollars following parental choice rather than *a priori* governmental assignment, we can fairly well predict that there will be occasional tensions between independent schools and the state sources of those tax dollars. We can predict that intrusiveness will threaten from time to time. But neither logic nor experience provide convincing reasons to believe that we must fall into the traps, succumb to the excess, and sacrifice the essential freedom of the independent sector. Indeed, a thoughtful voucher or scholarship program can enliven that independent sector, expand it, and in so doing provide at long last a comparative and competitive arena for state-owned schools.

There are a half-dozen major natural constituencies which, if alert, will join forces to break EFM in the several states, and replace it with educational choice. It will be a sad irony if those who most distrust state activity miss this opportunity to help control and shrink the state educational leviathan, today's most extreme case of governmental monopoly and overextension.

Choice Will Victimize (the Already Victimized)

The last of the false arguments against parental choice we will examine is in many respects the worst of all. I refer to the contention that parental choice would be the vehicle for abandoning the students trapped in failing inner-city schools. This goes under the heading of "creaming" or "skimming," usually, and is distinctively malicious because it makes pawns of the most unfortunate among us and, to do so, stands reality precisely on its head.

One of the standard forms of this charge is the assertion that school choice plans are in truth "not *parent* choice but *school* choice" provisions, that is, parents are not free to chose *any* private school, and private schools are free to deny students, ergo, school choice is a sham. The truth? When one day parents have *no* choice without financial penalty, and the next day they have *some* choice, some actual progress has been made, unless a half a loaf is truly no better than none. When the great bulk of private schools are not selective, and accept all applicants, and only a very few are selective and reject appreciable numbers—and that is the reality of things today—then real (though imperfect) parental choice has been introduced. And when such choice is provided, the effect is not further "abandonment" (of the already-abandoned). It is, instead, their best hope for salvation.

Far from aggravating the woeful status quo, wherein white flight has led to decimated neighborhoods and schools, given true choice parents and guardians are most likely to choose an independent school if their youngster is having trouble in public school, not if that youngster is excelling. On December 15, 1994, the *Milwaukee Sentinel* editorialized that "it must be a given" that under any choice system "some will be left behind in a system now minus the best and brightest children, who will have fled." Less than two months later, the same paper on February 8, 1995, reported on the results of the Legislative Audit Bureau's examination of this issue in the Milwaukee Parental Choice Program's experience: "Private schools taking part have not taken the brightest students from the Milwaukee Public Schools, as opponents feared." Exactly as logic would suggest, the report continued: "Instead, state auditors found that the average choice student had significantly worse scores on reading and math scores than other MPS students before the students transferred to private schools."

Ah, the facts. What devastation they wreak on faulty theory. What are the pertinent facts? The first and most obvious is that the students in the major inner-city public school systems are *already* "abandoned." They are the most obvious victims of the finance monopoly, the victims of violence and intimidation, declining graduation rates, and test scores. The second and overwhelming fact is that those same students would be the prime beneficiaries of a system of parental choice. In one motion such a system would give to inner-city parents and students one of the great privileges now reserved to those wealthy enough to pay for private schools: the capacity to choose from educational alternatives for their children, the chance finally to break the cycle of defeat that now confronts so many in the inner cities. That simple act of choice, creating a moral bond among parent-school-student, is the most dramatic entitlement and empowerment one can imagine providing to the most deprived of our citizens.

The overpowering truth of this is demonstrated most eloquently by this fact: survey after survey shows that the strongest support for parental choice comes from parents in the nation's central cities. They know how their welfare, and the welfare of their children, can be best satisfied. They know that the independent schools perform better, graduate their students better, see them on to college better. They know that the public schools now so often failing them will perform better for them if they are stripped of monopolistic protection and placed in a more competitive and responsive environment—if they are forced to be attractive enough to be *chosen* by newly empowered parents.

There is something very unsavory, if not malicious, about saying parental choice would lead to abandoning the already-abandoned, when it may well be their single greatest hope.

Parental Freedom

Now that we have dispelled some smoke and are able to view parental choice more clearly, what, in fact, do we see? What is most stunningly evident is that under a choice program we would see education proceeding naturally. We would see it, that is, able to form itself with a variety reflecting the models of education that naturally arise in a pluralistic society. Once we recognize this crucial fact, we should be able to resolve never again to let the argument over choice get stood on its head. Again we note: *It is not parental freedom that needs to justify itself, but any policy that limits it.*

We will see, too, that under a program of educational choice parental involvement in the schools—a universally acknowledged virtue—is greatly encouraged by the simple act of choice, as distinguished from "pupil assignment by the system." We will see at the same time that choice's dismantling of tendencies toward bureaucratic and program proliferation in today's monopolistic condition will serve to free teachers to teach—another precondition of excellent education. We will note the increased potential for morally charged educational alternatives, as the hold of the lowest-common-denominator monopoly is weakened.

We will see the inner-city disadvantaged suddenly able to purchase for their children educational options hitherto available only to the well off, and from this will come for those young people the real possibility of climbing out of poverty on the successive rungs of the education ladder. Not only will they benefit from the independent alternatives now available to them, but even more so from the newly responsive public schools that must appeal to them and sell themselves on the basis of comparative excellence. Those public schools, far from being attacked by parental choice, stand to benefit the most from it, if we are talking about educational quality rather than protection of vested interest.

When we see all this, we will see that education's twin objectives—personal empowerment and social strengthening—will be better met under conditions of parental choice than they can ever be under the prevailing system of monopoly financing. And then we can turn to sharing this good and definitive news with all the natural constituencies which will endorse choice when it is seen without obstruction. Once alerted and energized, they need only to be brought into networks of encouragement to and support for state government leaders who can discharge the simple but not easy last task: to break the stranglehold of those vested interests and hypnotized onlookers who, by deed and inertia, maintain monopolistic educational finance.

Since the smoke screens employed by EFM's defenders are standard and entirely predictable, one can expect to encounter them on every battlefield where parental freedom finally engages with educational finance monopoly. From many such engagements various astute observers have compiled not only lists of the usual smoke screens, but have written useful, often brief, refutations of those rhetorical efforts. From the many such efforts I will note only several which readers might want to consult. Particularly useful are chapter 11, "Common Criticisms of Privatization and Choice," in *American Education and the Dynamics of Choice*, by James R. Rinehart and Jackson F. Lee, Jr., New York, Praeger, 1991; chapter 3,

"Answering the Critics of School Choice," in *Education and Freedom*, by G. Dirk Mateer and Robert N. Mateer, Lynchburg, Virginia, CEBA, (1993); and Jeanne Allen's "Nine Lies About School Choice: Answering the Critics," Washington, Center for Educational Reform, 1994. Some of the material in this chapter was adapted from my own "Smoke Screens: How to Clear the Air on School Choice," *Wisconsin Interest*, Summer/Fall, 1992.

Do not imagine, however, that just dispelling such smoke screens solves the problem of how to achieve school choice. New smoke screens will be invented, whether it be witches or extremism or what have you. Indeed, it will be clear to all readers that rhetoric this hollow could not stand without assistance. That it has had much of, from political interests tied to the sources of these rhetorical ploys. Political muscle remains to defend what educational finance monopoly is really all about, that is, the protection of financial interests via monopoly controls intertwining with the political structure. So, to chapter 11 and a look at some of the political realities which up to now have obstructed school choice.

11

Why Are We in a Quagmire?
IV: The Political Tools of EFM's Defenders

Much of what has gone before in this volume points toward the truth of things: educational finance monopoly's ultimate defense has long been political control rather than the power of its arguments. This chapter will look a bit more particularly at how that political control has operated, and, also, at the new political realities which, finally, have put EFM at risk.

The most obvious factor to note in this context of control involves economic capacity to influence politics, as one would expect. The primary funds available to EFM defenders come from the union dues of the unionized educators. In their *Forbes* piece of June 7, 1993, "The National Extortion Association," Peter Brimelow and Leslie Spencer estimate the National Education Association's (NEA) dues derived income for the year at approximately $742 million. This vast total accumulates from national dues ($165 million), state educational association dues ($505 million), and local education association dues ($72 million). In *The NEA and the AFT: Teacher Unions in Power and Politics* (Rockport, Massachusetts, 1994), Charlene K. Haar, Myron Lieberman, and Leo Troy calculate the national-only dues for the following year, 1993–1994, at $173 million, drawing on the official NEA reports. The national American Federation of Teachers (AFT), for the year 1991–1992, was reported to have national dues-based income in excess of $67 million. If AFT national dues are in the same proportion to total dues as are the NEA's, then we could imagine total AFT dues based income at more than $300 million; and we can project total education union dues based income at more than $1 billion. Soon that could be serious money, as Senator Dirksen famously said about "a billion here, a billion there." It is the kind of money needed to advance the interests of politicians on whom EFM relies, buy important media time and space, and in general keep EFM's self-protective viewpoints constantly before the citizens' eyes.

The central task to which such funds are assigned is the task of maintaining the very monopoly from which the money comes. Keep the treasuries full by increasing the dues and increasing the contracts that provide the dollars to pay the dues, and do so essentially in a nonconfronted and noncompetitive environment. From such organization and treasuries come the programs that reinforce the funding status quo. It is that which advocates of school choice have to realize when they decide to go to battle. They need some countervailing resource base. It does not have to be identical. They do not need as much money as the defenders of EFM need, presumably, because there is still power in the truth and in the arguments for it. But inertia is there to be manipulated, and the dollars available to EFM's defenders are a large lever with which to do the manipulating.

Another source of strength for the defenders of EFM is the fact that state legislators have a normal, natural preoccupation with the ideas embodied in the words "education" and "youth." It is natural for politicians to be preoccupied with such qualities as those words convey. They have a desire to "do something," to "say something," about education. This is an important point, because the defenders of EFM have not only supplied dollars to the political machines of the nation, and they have not only supplied bodies, as seen below, but they have also supplied content. That is to say, they have provided fodder for the politicians to enable them to say something and to enable them to do something about youth and education. It is easy to forget that politicians are open to content suggestions on most of the things with which they deal, because it does not come naturally to them any more than it does to the rest of us to have pregnant ideas about the tremendous array of social subjects with which they have to deal. And thus it is that interested parties who have something to say and are articulate enough to say it, and have printing presses and copying machines that enable them to communicate with such groups as sitting state legislatures, have a leg up, if you wish, in the legislative process. There is nothing cynical about this. In many respects state legislators are books of blank pages waiting to be written on. So he who writes on them first often becomes definitive and part of the history of the impact and influence of the education finance monopoly defenders in this country is that they have seized the opportunity to provide content to state legislators. And this, again, is one of the things that those who oppose EFM and who want parental freedom and expanded school choice need to keep in mind. They need to help legislators in the various jurisdictions with categories and thoughts and content about education and youth.

We want, next, to note and consider the personnel contribution made by EFM defenders to the political processes of the fifty states and of the nation. The sheer numbers of union members, for example, in the National Education Association (NEA) and the American Federation of Teachers (AFT), simply make them a tremendous force within the political lives of fifty states. As reproduced in Lieberman, et al., at page 11, the *NEA 1993-94 Handbook* reported July 30, 1993 membership of 2,172,343. The same source, at page 24, reported that in 1993 the AFT claimed membership of 825,000. The two major educators' unions, thus, have combined membership of approximately 3 million as of 1993. These are mammoth numbers by any measure. And their distributed presence across the fifty states makes these unions major players in most jurisdictions. Given relatively large amounts of free time during non-teaching periods, these people represent volunteer political presence greater than any other social group without much question. They can sponsor and populate political programs and rallies, for example, more easily than most interest groups.

To illustrate much about the state-level political influence of education there is the celebrated case of Alabama, in which, thanks much to the work of the NEA, as of 1987 more than 40 percent of state legislators (58 out of 140) were identified as teachers, former teachers or spouses of teachers. Talk about dealer's control! (See Alan Ehrenhalt, *The United States of Ambition*, New York, 1991, and especially chapter 7 therein.) At the national level we see NEA and AFT members constituting 512 of 4,288 delegates (12 percent) at the 1992 Democratic convention (Lieberman, page 57), and that number no doubt would swell if the category were expanded to include family members, former members of NEA/AFT, and so on, as in the Alabama illustration. Whatever the exact number at the convention, one could see their impact when Governor Clinton referred to true school choice in baldly negative terms and vowed never to support it. And this was a candidate who, as governor of Arkansas, had seen the attractiveness of school choice, and had sought the advice of a premier school choice advocate, Wisconsin's State Representative Annette Polly Williams. Of course, as Arkansas Governor Clinton would have had little to fear in the NEA-AFT. But as Democratic presidential candidate, he quickly and easily became their obedient servant.

An even more stark demonstration of such servitude came the following year, before the national AFL-CIO convention in San Francisco. The AFT is an AFL-CIO affiliate, of course. Clinton's Labor Secretary informed the convention that "their agenda is our agenda." And before the AFL-CIO on Monday, October 4, 1993, President Clinton continued paying his dues. He advised California voters to oppose Proposition 174 and the educational choice it would provide. Once again he made clear that he does not see, or acknowledge, the manifest public policy questions implicit in his own cherished private school experience as a child and college student, and in the Clintons' choice of a private school for their daughter: should not parents generally have the same capacity? Should those parents be encouraged to choose and commit to schools, as Clinton and his mother did, or be discouraged and defeated by educational finance monopoly (EFM)?

His stated reasons for opposing educational choice without financial penalty were remarkable in several respects. They were, on the one hand, standard and commonplace smoke screens, everywhere used by choice opponents to obstruct citizens' vision. On the other hand, they were expressed in unusually exaggerated ways. As reported in the October 5, 1993, *White House Bulletin*, his first assertion—that Prop. 174 will "start by taking $1.3 billion" from public schools—was a form of the customary "siphon" argument. It suffered the usual "siphon" problems: contrary to his implications, choice does not say how many dollars public schools should get. Moreover, his comment presumed to know what no one knows: the exact relationship between educational cost and quality; and it put cart before horse, means above ends, by asking not of *education's* needs but of *public schools'* needs. His generally dysfunctional observation was especially inapt in the case of Prop. 174, of course, where the choice program proposed would not have applied at once to children already in private school.

His second sally was a scare tactic that ended up exalting bureaucracy over families. He asserted that Prop. 174 would authorize a kind of license: "Just take your voucher and who cares whether the private school is a legitimate school or not." "Who cares?" Indeed! *Parents* care, and that rather dramatically summarizes the fundamental dispute between educational choice advocates, on the one side, and those such as Mr. Clinton who defend educational finance monopoly on the other. A fundamental premise of choice is that most parents and guardians, loving their children and personally responsible for them, are more likely to seek and secure the welfare of those children than is any monopolistic bureaucracy. EFM's defenders, by contrast, cannot acknowledge parental authority and competence without endangering their own hegemony, and are driven instead to speak as if, absent monopolistic bureaucracy, no one will care for the child's welfare. That effectively dismisses parents, just as did Mr. Clinton's "Who cares?"

Mr. Clinton's final shot, in addition to being a rather strange way to repay the generosity of the Catholic schools that succored him, was one of the more extreme versions of using the church-state bogeyman to impede choice. He reflected on his own youthful years when Catholic schools were chosen by his non-Catholic mother to provide his educational nurturing, and those schools were generous enough to admit him. In those days, he told his audience, "no one ever thought that the church would want any money from the taxpayers to run their schools." It would be difficult to write a more blatantly discriminatory and error-filled statement than that: no church was demanding money under Prop. 174, and no church would have gotten money under it or any other serious school choice proposal. Not even church schools would directly receive such funds. Parent believers-as-citizens, of all faiths, would qualify for assistance now wrongfully denied them, as would parents of no faith. To impugn their right to seek such policy by pretending they are a "church" is in effect to say their religious faith makes them less than full citizens, unqualified to seek what others seek.

Whatever his motivations and self-understanding, Mr. Clinton in these passages engaged in a massive misportrayal of reality. He just made smoke, the classic maneuver when one has no ammunition to fire.

Not just national and state, but local politics, too, is heavily influenced by educators' unions. Particularly in low turnout elections such as off-year ballots, school board voting, and the like, they can be decisive "by the numbers," making up in disciplined turnout for any paucity of absolute numbers. And, because of relatively large budgets and time available, they can and do provide copious amounts of literature and voluntary voter workers. In school board elections, where the teachers' unions are often decisive participants, we then witness what amounts to the take over of the pertinent political apparatus by the group allegedly governed by that apparatus. Thus, as Peter Brimelow and Leslie Spencer observe in "Comeuppance" (*Forbes*, February 13, 1995) we get to see a monopoly (the unions) on top of a monopoly (the school boards controlling all education dedicated tax dollars). And that, it should be clear, is just another name for my educational finance monopoly, or EFM.

The political muscle developed by such financial and personal resources was nicely displayed in the case of Proposition 174 in 1993 in California. Proposition 174 was a substantial school choice initiative that, had it been approved, would have inaugurated limited school choice statewide in the Golden State. It was, of course, the natural enemy of the NEA and the AFT and of their local equivalents, the California Teachers Association (CTA) and California Federation of Teachers (CFT). From what we have seen already, we know that EFM's self-interested defenders have extremely large and predictable funding sources; they have very large numbers of members, voluntary workers, and professional staff; and they have very close ties to the political order, media and allied organizations. Such are the ingredients of a recipe for political strength and political success. Perhaps there is no recent example better than the 1993 defeat of California's Proposition 174 to illustrate how such muscle can be utilized when all is going right for educational finance monopoly. The whole story is summarized very effectively in Lieberman, et al., pages 71-80, as it was in the *Los Angeles Times* and *San Francisco Chronicle* during 1993, and I will just touch on a few points here.

Proposition 174 had a variety of vulnerabilities which made it relatively easy to attack. Moreover, it was a "one step," "all at one time," effort involving referendum and constitutional change and specific school choice proposal in one motion. Given this, one could not convincingly say of its flaws: "Don't worry. We'll fix those next time around," as one could say of a legislative equivalent. Put its substantive problems with its procedural ones, and one can think of Proposition 174 as relatively "easy pickin's." But even had it been a much less vulnerable proposal than it was, it would have had trouble overcoming the onslaught against it from EFM's core defenders, the NEA, AFT, and their California subsidiaries.

The advocates and sponsors of Proposition 174, loosely organized and funded at around $2.5 million, were simply destroyed by the tightly structured EFM defenders numbering over 225,000 in the CTA alone, and aided and abetted by thousands of California PTA members representing the total membership of California PTA of approximately 1 million. (*Los Angeles Times*, October 25, 1993) Thousands of PTA members, for example, manned untold numbers of phonebanks aimed at blocking support for Proposition 174. And all the state level groups were, in turn, counseled and supported by the national offices of the NEA and the AFT. Over and above such massive contributions of time and effort, according to Lieberman, et al., at page 74, the CTA political action committees (PACs) raised more than $18 million to oppose Proposition 174. This enabled them to afford massive purchases of television and radio time, newspaper ads, the very high cost devices a referendum calls for, to get a broadbased public effectively targeted. Such expensive devices were essentially beyond the reach of Proposition 174 advocates.

Through such displays of financial and political strength, arrayed against a weak, underfunded and ill-organized foe, EFM turned what had been shallow but real majority support for Proposition 174 into a 70 percent to 30 percent rout at the polls on November 2, 1993. But, as the Luntz-Weber exit polls made plain, even as they slaughtered a Proposition 174 they had been taught to fear, California voters appreciated, and desired by a margin of nearly 3-1, choice at the conceptual level, as we have previously seen.

For more routine and sustained political purposes, EFM over the years has forged political triangles in most states. The triangles consist, on the one side, of educational unions and their supporters; on another side the educational bureaucratic structures characteristic of most states, whether they be called departments of education or departments of public instruction, organizations which have traditionally been part and parcel of educational finance monopoly; and on the third side, liaison with state legislative and administrative power structures, especially the education committees of state legislatures, the traditional burying grounds of anything threatening financial monopoly, including any or all choice initiatives.

But of course there is a flip side to living by political protection. If defense of EFM is truly by political power rather than substantive and rationally defensible arguments for it, then what happens to EFM if its power base is lost? It still has inertia to use, of course, and knee-jerk reactions of support from, for example, statist-oriented press, the ACLU, and traditional supporters of educational finance monopoly and opponents of parental rights. It still has available also the "last refuge of political scoundrels": that is, because of the American habit of judicial review, it has the courts to try to block legislative judgment. But, essentially, if the usual political controls are lost, there is a potential for great change, not a little. What has happened in the wake of the November 8, 1994, elections is not a little change in the conditions confronting educational finance monopoly but a great deal of change. In many states, EFM defenders lost more than just a few seats. They lost their power base itself. This is easily seen abstractly, for given one-party identification, as in many places, new power holders, even if neutral toward school choice, owe EFM nothing but the figurative back of the hand. What do I mean by one-party identification? An illustration may suffice: in the 1992 elections the NEA's political action committee supported thirty-nine U.S. Senate candidates—thirty-eight Democrats, one Republican (Lieberman, et al., p. 85). When party support is that lopsided, the supporting organization cannot afford change of power.

But beyond abstraction, the elections of November 8, 1994, actually had a revolutionary impact on the struggle against EFM and the struggle for parental freedom. I have written much about the need for school choice workers in the various states to help create a countervailing power to offset the entrenched and self-interested defenders of educational finance monopoly. EFM's long-standing accumulation of staff, finances, and linkage to state legislative and executive power means that advocates of parental freedom need to break the grip of such controls, and make school choice both safe for and attractive to state politicians.

What was the general impact of the November 8 elections as regards breaking the control of EFM, making school choice safe for politicians, and gaining momentum for that parent-serving and justice-serving policy? As the following descriptions will make plain, school choice and America's parents were huge winners on November 8. After that election there were sitting governors in more states than ever who were on record in support of school choice and parental freedom, as contrasted with EFM's status quo. Victory for such candidates established this liberating fact: EFM's bureaucratic and union grasp on state power could be broken. There are now unprecedented numbers of state-level decision-makers, executive and legislative, who owe nothing politically to EFM's defenders.

These are facts. They are *potent* facts. They were not, however, victory for school choice. But that victory could be much more easily achieved after and because of the November 8 elections. This represented great progress and genuine momentum built up in recent years in many states. After the election, an observer could see that if only a few of those states granted parents' rights to school choice, the snowball might be started down the hill. Parents in neighboring states could be expected to demand the freedom their neighbors had achieved. Space will not permit a comprehensive picture of November 8 results pertinent to school choice, but some of the highlights follow.

Pennsylvania

After the November 8 elections, Republican Congressman and school choice advocate Tom Ridge would become the next governor of Pennsylvania. In the election, Mr. Ridge decisively defeated the Democratic candidate and current Lieutenant Governor Mark Singel, by more than 200,000 votes, and he did so despite the fact that there are 500,000 more registered Democratic than Republican voters in the state. He also defeated independent candidate Peg Luksik whose strong support for parental rights and educational choice via tax credits likely drew a good number of votes away from Mr. Ridge. Final tallies showed that Tom Ridge won 45 percent of votes cast, while Mark Singel and Peg Luksik gained 40 percent and 13 percent, respectively. (*Pittsburgh Post-Gazette*, November 11, 1994; *New York Times*, November 10, 1994)

Both Mr. Ridge and Mr. Singel advocated charter schools and choice within the public school system during their campaigns. But while Mr. Singel stated that he would staunchly oppose any school choice proposal that included private schools among the options available to families, Mr. Ridge made comprehensive choice in education a major theme in his campaign and declared that he "would work to give parents the right to choose the school their child attends, including private and religious schools" (*Philadelphia Inquirer*, October 27, 1994). Mr. Ridge proposed that education voucher programs be established initially in the neediest parts of the state. Mr. Singel's firm opposition to comprehensive choice gained him the endorsements of the state's public school teachers' unions, the Pennsylvania State Education Association and the Pennsylvania Federation of Teachers, both of which contributed huge sums of money to his campaign. Mr. Ridge, on the other hand, received the endorsement of Pennsylvania's REACH (Road to Educational Achievement through Choice) Political Action Committee (*Pittsburgh Post-Gazette*, October 27, 1994; *Harrisburg Patriot News*, October 2, 1994).

Ohio

Breaking the state's record for margin of victory in a gubernatorial contest, incumbent Governor George Voinovich overwhelmed his Democratic opponent, Robert Burch, in the November 8 election. Governor Voinovich gained 72 percent of the votes cast to Mr. Burch's 25 percent. (*Cleveland Plain Dealer,* November 9, 1994; *New York Times,* November 10, 1994) Governor Voinovich is a supporter of parental choice in education and had earlier established a commission to explore educational choice options. From that commission came the Ohio Scholarship Plan, a proposal to allow a limited number of school districts in the state to implement pilot school choice programs. The proposal, backed by the governor, was introduced in the state legislature; but the effort eventually failed after House leadership assigned the bill to a then-hostile Education Committee. The recent general election in Ohio brought not only a victory for the governor, however. It resulted also in Republican control of both the state's House and Senate. School choice advocates in Ohio knew that the Ohio Scholarship Plan would be reintroduced in the state legislature, and that Governor Voinovich would make provisions for the plan in his forthcoming executive budget. With committee chairmanships now controlled by members of the Governor's own party, the Ohio Scholarship Plan's chances had improved considerably.

Wisconsin

Seeking a third term as governor, Republican Tommy Thompson easily defeated his Democratic opponent, state Senator Chuck Chvala. Governor Thompson won 67 percent of the total vote. (*Milwaukee Journal,* November 9, 1994) Governor Thompson, a well-known supporter of educational choice, signed into law in 1990 the original Milwaukee Parental Choice Program, the program championed by Democratic State Represetative Annette Polly Williams. As in Ohio, Thompson's landslide victory was accompanied by State Republican legislators winning control of both the Assembly and the Senate. Governor Thompson could anticipate greater cooperation from a legislature controlled by those more sympathetic to his agenda. The election results prompted a teachers' union official to remark, "Given the new political realities, it's even more important the MTEA (Milwaukee Teachers' Education Association) moves swiftly to embrace reform and pushes its members to do likewise" (*Milwaukee Journal,* November 10, 1994).

Note, also, that in the November 8, 1994, election the Republicans seized control of the House of Representatives and the Senate of the United States and began a substantial series of changes pertinent to EFM there, as well. And there were many other states in addition to the ones cited here in which the climate changed, for example, Connecticut and Arizona, but they were less well developed in terms of planning, coalition construction, and so on. The cases of electoral results here summarized are also the cases I will follow for school choice. Regarding Pennsylvania, we can say there was a substantial political revolution in that state. The election of a governor, Tom Ridge, who is strongly supportive of school choice and willing to put his political life to work in support of that reformation was of major importance. In six months he transformed the political debate within Pennsylvania. He was not finally successful in securing passage of a statewide school choice initiative in Pennsylvania in spring, 1995, but he came very close, winning in the Senate and losing in the lower house of the Pennsylvania legislature by a relatively few votes, 106 to 95. Lack of success appeared to come only because Governor Ridge had been in office too short a period of time to achieve disciplined response by his own party in the lower house of the legislature. He and his colleagues are expected to revisit school choice.

A second case beyond abstraction is the activity going on within the confines of the United States Congress, and that activity takes two forms in two directions. First, there is substantial consideration being given to incorporating a form of school choice into the general reform of the District's educational performance which, of course, has been a human disaster for years. So, on one level, precisely because of November 8th, we have the vision of a newly energized school choice-oriented majority in Congress, willing to look for ways to find choice adaptations that will help rescue the dire and disastrous conditions of the District. At the very same time in the form of the Coats-Lieberman legislation in the Senate and the companion Riggs-Weldon legislation in the House of Representatives, we have Congress also giving serious consideration to pilot programs funded by federal dollars that would support school choice initiatives at the local level around the country. These are two very vital signs. Only time will tell to what degree the Washington-based efforts will be successful, but the point is that the November 8th elections created a whole new set of potentials and possibilities which did not exist before.

Ohio

Still examining the impact of that November 8, 1994, election, we turn to Ohio and specifically the city of Cleveland. Governor Voinovich emerged from the November 8th elections with a whopping majority, as we saw, and tremendous support among minority communities in the major cities of the state. Governor Voinovich had previously signaled that he was supportive of school choice experimentation. And those supportive of school choice achieved majorities in both houses of the Cleveland legislature. And as a result, school choice promoters were able during the spring of 1995, in late June, specifically, to achieve passage of a Cleveland pilot program of genuine choice in the state of Ohio. This represents one of the first breakthroughs of true school choice legislation on the mainland.

Wisconsin

Running on a parallel path with Ohio, but of somewhat larger import because it is a much more substantial program, was Wisconsin. Again, November 8th was decisive. There was already in office a Republican governor interested in school choice advancements. There was a Senate controlled seventeen to sixteen by the governor's own party and thus potentially available to support school choice if the Assembly could be brought in line. And, as a result of the November 8 election, the Assembly of the Wisconsin legislature joined the Senate and the governor with a Republican majority. Thus, the whole configuration of politics in that state was revolutionized by the November 8th election. Revolutionized, that is, in the form of the transfer of power within the Wisconsin Assembly, even though only a few seats changed hands. (The point of all this is not partisan, of course. Many of the most eloquent and impressive school choice spokesmen are prominent Democrats. The point, rather, is the loss of power by EFM defenders and the growth in power of those who would promote, or at least not obstruct, parental freedom via school choice.)

It probably is true that there can be no better illustration of the fact that EFM is a substantively hollow structure clutching to power for financial advantage than the case of Wisconsin, 1995. Here EFM suffered its most prominent mainland defeat up to this writing. It could quite possibly be the beginning of EFM's ultimate demise if "parent envy" and "city envy" join other dynamics aimed at basic funding change. In other words, it will be the beginning of EFM's end if the school choice fever is spread by such sayings as, "If Milwaukee can have it, why can't we?"

And, in Wisconsin, with stunning clarity, almost as in a laboratory experiment, we have seen on what the issue turned. Wisconsin has long been a school choice hotbed and thus a place in which enormous human effort has been expended over the last thirty-five years. The net effect of that, no doubt, was to bring greater legitimacy to the concept of parental freedom than exists in most places. Greater exposure of the emptiness of EFM's smoke screens, as well, has occurred by the steady and widespread efforts of many to dispel them. Over time, such efforts have had an impact on developing a climate more tolerant of the "radical" concept of parents' allocation of some educational dollars. The evolution of the thinking of the Metropolitan Milwaukee Association of Commerce (MMAC) from 1991 onward, and its 1993 elevation of choice to the top of its legislative agenda is an example of how things have developed in the state of Wisconsin, and it is also a crucially important thing in itself. For what it did was to inject a substantial funding source to support the effort to achieve school choice for Milwaukee. The program is geographically and means tested, and is, thus, limited. But, nonetheless, it is genuine school choice achieved through the vehicle of expanding the Milwaukee Parental Choice Program to include religious schools and greatly increasing the number of eligible students.

A long history of school choice activity in Wisconsin, a history with many heroes, seemed to prepare the soil. Yet, when all is said and done, the pivot, the fact that built on but went beyond all other facts that preceded it, was the November 8, 1994, transfer of power in the Wisconsin Assembly from a Democratic majority, the primary political support and defender of EFM in the political arena and in all likelihood the blocker of MPCP expansion if the Democratic majority had not been lost; to a new Republican majority which not only *owed* EFM nothing, but actually had some contempt for it. Through such vehicles as Wisconsin Educational Association Council (WEAC), EFM had long been a tormentor of Republican aspirants for state-level office. When those long-suffering "outs" became the "ins," there was not just a shift of a few seats, but a complete collapse of the traditional power base supporting EFM.

From November, 1994 to now, and especially after the governor on January 14, 1995 made known his intentions to include MPCP expansion in his executive budget, the defensive smoke screens thrown up by EFM became at once shriller *and* weaker day by day, as the realization of what truly had happened began to sink in. The president of the Wisconsin Education Association Council threatened to organize private school teachers if MPCP were expanded to include true choice. (*Milwaukee Jour-*

nal Sentinel, March 31, 1995) The Superintendent of the Department of Public Instruction accused the Governor of "sacrific[ing] the school system" through malevolent "sabotage." (Ibid., January 19, January 27, and March 3, 1995) The President of the Wisconsin Coalition for Public Education claimed MPCP expansion would directly fund witchcraft and "hate" schools. (*Capital Times,* January 16, 1995) And, after a number of local businesses publicly showed support for school choice in a newspaper ad, WEAC's president threatened them with the equivalent of a boycott in a March 22nd letter to community leaders. Shriller *and* weaker. I thought during those times, often, of the Wicked Witch of the West in *The Wizard of Oz* shriveling up when she had water thrown on her. That is akin to what EFM's classic defenders looked and sounded like in the period from November 8th to the end of June, 1995, when MPCP expansion, with the incorporation of true school choice, happened in Wisconsin.

What these descriptions show is that what happened on November 8, 1994, in Wisconsin and in other jurisdictions was not the loss of a few seats, but a decisive loss of political control and this has led to increasing exposure of what EFM has used to defend itself, namely political control, not educational merit. This is a fight over political control, not over education. What is at stake are dollars protected by the finance monopoly serving the perceived welfare of a unique interest group. Again, there is nothing evil about this; nothing even surprising. But there is absolutely no reason for disinterested parties to support that kind of program.

Now that we have several-sided knowledge of why we are stuck in the educational quagmire, we can in chapter 12 identify some of the steps best used to get out of that condition.

Part IV

The Many Paths to Parental Freedom and School Choice

12

Parental Freedom via School Choice: Getting There From Here

In chapter 1 we showed how simply and naturally we could fashion a policy of school choice without financial penalty, if we were starting from a "state of nature." Our policymakers (not "professional" vested interests) would ask and answer several obvious questions: what are the educational objectives against which educational providers can be evaluated? Should parents' rights and capabilities match their responsibilities? Are they responsible for the nurturing of their children, including their educational formation? Do we want educational funding policy to support and encourage parents in exercising their responsibility for the child's welfare? Do we want to encourage family integrity, and the understanding of the school as an extension of, and partner with, the family? And do we want to create a funding environment in which all schools can be compared and can be judged rationally as to relative performance, and thus be stimulated to both excellence and efficiency? If able to see clearly, responsible policymakers, and the citizens they represent, would answer each of these questions with a resounding "Yes!"

Having so seen and answered, they would decide how much tax money should be deployed to these objectives and then say: let the tax dollars follow parents' choice of educational environment, for, of all social entities, the parents most desire, and are most likely to seek, the welfare of their children. That is the obvious and overriding rationale for this assignment of tax dollars dedicated to education, when citizens and policymakers are able clearly to see the natural logic of parental and social responsibility. And, far from being a utopian scheme, what has been described here is essentially what is done in more educationally enlightened nations around the world, for example, Denmark, Holland, Australia. And it is done in such places to the great satisfaction of parents, with excellent educational results, and at less cost than we pay to do education badly in the United States.

Thus, what we talk of as ideal policy if seen from a "state of nature" is, as well, a practical description of how various nations actually handle and solve the problems of educational funding. Part of the ease with which many nations have solved this problem stems from the fact that they have been able to disburse funds directly to independent schools, including religious schools. Their ability to fund school choice that way simply reflects the fact that, unlike the United States, they are not saddled with judicially imposed church-state interpretations that obstruct state-school contacts. Given the existence of such impediments in the United States, the obvious path to school choice here is through the disbursement of education-dedicated tax dollars via parents, rather than to schools. Hence, naturally and correctly, all substantial school choice efforts now ongoing in the United States feature the funding of *parents'* choices, not schools, via vouchers, scholarships, or tax credits. Such approaches clearly pass the tests of common sense and federal judicial interpretation rules as established especially in the *Witters v. Department of Services for the Blind,* 474 U.S. 481 (1986), *Mueller v. Allen,* 463 U.S. 388 (1983), and *Zobrest v. Catalina Foothills School District,* 113 S. Ct. 2462 (1993) decisions. Also regarding the question of constitutional impediments, see Clint Bolick and Richard D. Komer's "School Choice: Answers to the Most Frequently Asked Legal Questions," *Institute for Justice,* 1994.

Fifty States: Fifty Jobs to be Done

But church-state complications are only a part, indeed, a small part, of the problem of achieving educational choice in the United States. The much larger difficulty resides in the fact that it must be achieved fifty times, in fifty jurisdictions, each of which has its own particular history and context. And, in each of these jurisdictions, the school choice effort must proceed not with a clean slate but from the captivity of social inertia—the habits of a long-entrenched system, able to be manipulated effectively by the vested interests that benefit from it.

Having spent several years examining the efforts to free parents in many states, it has become clear to me that one of the greatest allies of EFM's defenders is the sense of frustration that has so often beset, and enervated, so many school choice workers. In one sense, such frustration is understandable, for the path to overcoming EFM, though plain enough, is most assuredly a difficult one. They must identify the natural constituency groups in society whose interests would be better served by educational choice than by EFM. These natural constituencies of choice include, for example, all parents concerned for educational excellence impeded by EFM; those concerned for growing ethical separation between home and school; inner-city parents seeing failing schools for their children; taxpayers' alliances who know the inefficiencies of monopoly; business groups worried about workforce quality in an increasingly competitive world, et al. Choice advocates must help these groups see their interests, and help them see the need for coalition. For standing alone they have no chance of success, but if standing together they cannot be stopped. They have enough political mass to make their weight effectively insuperable.

A few breakthroughs in a few states will likely have a snowball effect. Parents, seeing their neighbors' freedom to decide their child's educational environment, are very likely to want that same capacity for themselves. The status quo probably would begin quickly to lose the inertial presumption which now sustains it. But until those things are done, until those breakthroughs are achieved in fact, it is simply not helpful to refer, as many spokesmen repeatedly do, to the alleged inevitability of educational choice. The fact of the matter is there is nothing inevitable about it in any given jurisdiction, as things now stand. If it is not done right, if the political task is not done from the ground up and fundamentally, then the status quo can be sustained for an indefinite period of time, because its defenders will continue to exploit social inertia successfully against all puny and superficial attacks. Choice advocates' zeal, if based on a too-simple political analysis, too easily becomes frustration, and the frustration inadvertently can become a reinforcement of the circularity of the contemporary situation. There is no justification for that frustration, for it simply means that the persons experiencing it did not see the severity of the problem at the beginning. There is no time like the present to get a better grasp of what it takes to achieve basic change in this crucial area. America's children need it and America's parents deserve it.

Recognizing the local, very concrete, and very particular nature of the problem (the fifty problems) will serve as a useful reminder, also, of how alert school choice advocates need to be to the sensibilities of parents in each jurisdiction. Vested interest defenders of the status quo, whose material welfare is tied up with it, should be seen for what they are and be called by the right name. We know that even they are not demons, of course, for people naturally defend the spigot from which they drink, and tend not to transcend their material and personal interests. Parents and other groups that are brought on as unsuspecting allies of vested interests—the PTAs, school boards and such, which we call the "altruistic corollaries" of EFM's vested interests—are different, however.

"Altruistic Corollaries," Dispelling Smoke, and Following the North Star

Until they can see clearly, when the smoke screens have been dispersed, altruistic supporters of EFM, and the politicians representing them, are naturally concerned that any change from the status quo should be gradual, ensuring that the current system (to which their children are assigned, for instance) not suffer even as new parental freedom is achieved. School choice advocates know that school choice will benefit all children by stimulating all schools to make themselves choiceworthy. But for many citizens and parents, all that they know about is the status quo.

Given that, and given financial realities and limitations, it is quite natural that school choice proposals from prudent people will feature gradual, phase-in approaches. These can give assurance to people of good will that, even as the system of educational funding begins fundamentally to change from EFM to increasing parental control, the interests of the children now in EFM's schools will be safeguarded. Similarly, state governments will benefit from assurance that any start-up costs associated with the adoption of school choice, in due time if not immediately, will be more than offset by the combination of efficiencies and excellence which school choice can and will deliver. Particularly useful for those people who have progressed to a full understanding of school choice's liberating power, is this caution: not everyone with whom they will need to work will have progressed so far. Many people will have an inclination toward school choice, and strong instincts against monopoly, but still carry much inertial baggage. "Patience, people."

As the specific school choice plans discussed in chapter 7 make plain, there are many ways to reconcile these interests and sensitivities, and at the same time keep moving resolutely toward the North Star of parental control over educational funding. It is absolutely essential, however, even if gradual models for implementing genuine school choice are used to ease the impact on the status quo and to achieve peace of mind for the captives of inertia, that choice advocates at all costs avoid the logical trap of confusing ends and means. "Even if educational finance monopoly is destructive to parents and students, don't disturb EFM!" That is the trap of confusing ends and means. That is the trap of beginning with the assumption that whatever else we do, we must somehow guarantee the essential outlines of what we have. That approach has to be rejected out of hand, for, if succumbed to, it essentially paralyzes its victims.

Consider, again, for example, one of the standard defenses of EFM, referred to several times in this volume: "Educational choice must be opposed, for it will siphon funds from the already-hurting public schools." This smoke screen suffers in many ways. As we know, choice as such says nothing about the number of dollars to be spent on public schools. Moreover, the "siphon" charge entirely begs the question as to the relationship between school expenditure and school quality. But worst of all, the siphon contention is misleading and destructive of rational discourse, because it elevates public schools to the status of ends-in-themselves, rather than what they are in fact: alternate means to the good end of education. If elevated to ends-in-themselves, such schools cannot be evaluated and compared with alternate providers, and are essentially beyond control. One of the major confusions in the debate over school choice is represented by this "siphon" theme. Parental freedom, it is routinely said, will harm the public schools, or is aimed at the public schools. As we have made clear, such is not the case. When it is rightly understood as a reform of funding methods, it is worth repeating, *school choice is school neutral and parent positive*. Conceived of as educational providers, rather than as fortresses protecting financial interests, America's public schools are likely to be the prime beneficiaries of school choice for the indefinite future.

Approaching Genuine Choice: A Litmus Test

One can accept, even welcome, gradual approaches to educational choice, not because choice is experimental and certainly not because it is a radical program, but simply to ease the transition for any and all persons now tied to the status quo, and to help policymakers deal with the financial aspects of moving from EFM to parental freedom.

The test, then, of any serious reform in the direction of educational choice is this: is the *telos* or end of the reform crystal clear, no matter the number of steps taken to it? What does crystal clear mean? It means essentially the following three points:

1. Is educational finance monopoly being dismantled, even if it has been decided to have several steps in the process?
2. Are parents becoming the assigners of some or all of tax dollars dedicated to education, enough first to lessen and finally to remove the penalty attached to making a choice?
3. Can the family's values, including religious values, be sought in the chosen school, thereby encouraging schools to be an extension and surrogate of the family?

Those are the questions which must be answered affirmatively as the basic test for any acceptable, truly dynamic or substantial reform in the direction of educational choice. The rest of the test is politically evident: does the proposed program take the process as far as political realities permit at the time?

Dispelling smoke and making it possible for others to do so is an essential part of achieving school choice and parental freedom. Knowing the weight of social inertia and the willingness of vested interests to exploit that inertia is also a vital part of achieving school choice. And knowing something of the resultant political liaisons—and the risks thereof—provides the remaining ingredients for the recipe of how to get to the promised land: parental freedom via school choice without financial penalty. How to do it is implicit in all that we have seen.

So, what we are talking about is political action to change educational funding policies in fifty states from educational finance monopoly, EFM, to school choice without financial penalty and the parental freedom that it would provide. That is the objective which we have been pursuing. What is needed to achieve this objective? A first need is political leadership able to galvanize pertinent constituencies to symbolize the issue and make it concrete. That may be a Wisconsin Senator John Plewa, or it may be Milwaukee Mayor John Norquist who has migrated to full school choice, or it may be Jersey City Mayor Bret Schundler or Pennsylvania Governor Tom Ridge or Wisconsin Representative Annette Polly Williams or Wisconsin Governor Tommy Thompson or Missouri Senator Peter Kinder or Kansas Representative Kay O'Connor or Florida Representative Stephen Wise, to mention just a few of the more effective political leaders of the school choice movement. In any case, the task of achieving the actual overcoming of EFM and its replacement with school choice needs, and will prosper from, political stalking horses of the kind here described. Such people are able in their persons and in their personalities to make very concrete the issues involved in the choice between educational finance monopoly and parental freedom. A second need, and these are all related needs, naturally, is for a political climate which, over time, legitimizes school choice, blows away the smoke screens defending educational finance monopoly, strips EFM down to the financial reality that it is, an effort to protect financial advantage through political controls.

Again emphasizing the integrated and related nature of these things, what is achieved by such political legitimization is the fulfillment of yet another need: to provide a kind of immunity for the politicians who will finally have to act against the educational funding status quo. Looked at from another perspective, what we are talking about here is giving the politicians of a given state something else to be concerned about, not just the traditional defenders of EFM, the education unions, and so on, but something else about which to be sensitive and responsive. It is necessary to remove the fear of the old forces and provide new motives to the state's politicians to act in favor of parental freedom and the equation of parental responsibility and obligation.

In this situation, and understanding these needs, one can see the great advantages that can flow from an umbrella organization within a given state, which organization can carry on the legitimization and rhetorical needs of the school choice effort. It can alert and sensitize the natural constituencies of choice discussed above. It can provide a unifying umbrella under which those constituencies can unite, and can see a good greater than their own. This role of changing the rhetorical climate and immunizing politicians is one an umbrella organization for school choice can greatly help achieve. It can also help facilitate the liaisons between school choice constituencies and political power. It can lead the several constituencies to agree on a specific vehicle for the policy of school choice. It can help teach the hard truth that "the duration" is the only rational time frame to talk about because an organization, unlike individuals, has a kind of continuing character to it and is less prone to enthusiasm-deflation than individuals standing alone may well be. And, furthermore, a school choice umbrella organization can sustain the effort for school choice after the initial breakthrough because, as we can see clearly from our analysis up to this point, the initial breakthrough will not be the end of the school choice evolution required in a given state. It may well be that the beginning of school choice, if in the form of a very limited program such as MPCP expansion, simply creates a better climate for the ultimate victory of school choice; and to exploit that climate one needs a *sustaining* organization, not an *ad hoc* organization whose logic has expired in the achievement of some very partial choice program.

Thus, for example, if we look at the Wisconsin effort concentrated on MPCP expansion or if we look at the Pennsylvania effort concentrated on a very severely dollar-limited and means-tested choice program, we recognize immediately that, excellent as both of those efforts have been, they do not exhaust nor complete the logic of school choice. They really only begin the unfolding of that logic. And, therefore, the very nature of those programs, once again, indicates the desirability of a continuing organization, such as that theoretically defined in the Wisconsin PACE (Parents Acquiring Choice in Education) effort; or Pennsylvania's REACH (Road to Educational Achievement Through Choice) Alliance, for example.

Naturally, we do not submit politics and political reality to organizational needs; just the reverse. Political reality rules. If a short cut presents itself, and it becomes possible to telescope certain historical stages that might otherwise be necessary, then school choice advocates obviously should take that short cut. The one thing to be cautious of is not to buy out too early, such as appears to have happened, for example, in the case of Michigan where one of the strongest school choice efforts for a time was derailed by the willingness of certain political leaders to settle for charter school initiatives. It may be, of course, that the charter school movement properly understood can be itself a step toward school choice, as we have seen above. But left to its own devices it does not take us in that direction in any necessary sense, and therefore it can be, in fact, a detour and a devastatingly bad one. So, we recognize prudence; we recognize partial steps. We move from the imperfect to the more perfect. That is the usual path of democratic politics and that is a powerful reason why a sustaining organization is necessary: because a state's original school choice effort is certainly unlikely to be a perfect or ultimate school choice design.

Today, thanks to the efforts of countless people, we have school choice activities and organizations in more than forty states, and notably strong school choice activities ongoing in a dozen and a half states or so. Of these, six or seven are very hot spots, and, as we know, two of these have already achieved limited but genuine school choice victories. Even as this book is being written, with the two breakthroughs and the several others close to success, it is possible to see the nationwide political calculus beginning to change, if only slowly. Choice programs in being will attack the "experimental" myth. They will in short order give the lie to the scare myths, and the other traditional diversions used to block parental freedom up to now. We can expect the programs to work well, despite their limitations, and we already know that parents welcome and endorse their new freedom and will not under any circumstances want to relinquish it. This fact, when seen by other parents in other locales and in other income strata, is the most powerful reality likely to begin fundamental change in the political calculus which hitherto has obstructed school choice. Totally legitimate "parent envy" can be expected to lead to totally legitimate parent questions and demands: "If *they* can have freedom for their children's education, why can't *we*?" The potential for this explains the desperate statements of EFM defenders as the passage of Milwaukee's expanded choice program was nearing its conclusion: "If they [poor Milwaukee parents] get this freedom, parents all around the state will want it!"

Some Examples of Alternative State-Level "Starter" Programs

If we assume the political climate of a given jurisdiction is ready for a statewide program rather than a pilot or local option design, then the Florida, Kansas and New York models are very useful. Florida's HJR 39 ("G.I. Bill for Florida Students") would have amended the State Constitution to allow K-12 students to use state funds at any accredited Florida schools. This is a simple, beautifully crafted resolution designed to provide aid to parents and families, not schools, not churches, and not any established religion. It obliterates the faulty church-state smoke screen.

In Kansas, Representative Kay O'Connor's 1994 HB 2754, as its 1995 successor, HB 2217, was a phase-in proposal in which the number of families eligible to receive vouchers to be used at only locally recognized private schools would gradually increase over five years. The amount of the voucher, at first equal to 50 percent of the state's per-pupil expenditure, would also gradually increase over five years.

New York's S. 5955 1995 phase-in proposal also would have begun gradually, allowing families with incomes in the lowest one-third in the state to qualify for $1,700 vouchers (approximately 20 percent of per-pupil state cost), and by the third year, all families would have been allowed to participate with vouchers amounting to approximately 40% of public school cost, or $3,400.

These Kansas and New York phase-in proposals, and others like them, are directly aimed at arguments against vouchers which occurred repeatedly in the Colorado and California debates. These arguments claimed that up-front costs of implementation would inevitably damage public education by depleting its "already-skimpy" coffers. The Kansas and New York responses show clearly that a *gradual* implementation can have a long-range *cost-savings* effect on state education budgets, and *at least* not a serious negative financial impact in its early stages of implementation. Even more important, of course, true school choice will encourage budgetary *rationality* by making comparison of alternate school types possible and eliminating the "budgeting in a vacuum" that necessarily occurs under EFM. That is the automatic promise of school choice. Ironically enough, if true choice helped restore public confidence in school funding, it might in some places encourage greater school provisions, including provisions for public schools.

As noted previously, Florida's proposal is especially well equipped to handle another of the commonly raised smoke screens in that education dollars are given so pointedly to *parents* and *families*, not schools. It is, after all, the "G.I. Bill for Florida Students." One element of Florida's HB 1021 particularly effectively attacks the church-state hobgoblin so often employed by choice opponents. What follows is Section 8 of HB 1021.

> Certificates are grants-of-aid to children through their parents, not to the schools in which the children are enrolled. The selection by parents of a school shall not constitute a decision or act of the state or any of its subdivisions. Payment to a religious or parochial school for educational services under this act shall not constitute aid to any church, sect, religious denomination, or sectarian institution.

This fine, plain assertion of legislative intent states the simple reality of things: certificates or vouchers assigned by parents have nothing to do with the state establishing or interfering with a church, no more than does a social security recipient spending some of his check to pay cabfare to church. Long live the declarative sentence!

If a tax credit approach is taken instead of a scholarship or grant approach, then Wisconsin's SB 310 of 1993 had much to commend it. It met many of the objections which defenders of the *status quo* have raised against choice methods. Wisconsin's SB 310 was designed to provide tax credits to parents to recover expenses incurred for their K-12 children's education up to $1,000 per child. The tax credits could have been claimed for tuition at private or parochial schools. Parents who did not pay state taxes equivalent to the credits for which they qualified would receive state checks to make up the difference.

If prevailing political realities suggest that a pilot or local option approach is the appropriate way to begin school choice in a given jurisdiction, then the Ohio, New Jersey, Connecticut, and Milwaukee Parental Choice Program expansion proposals, among others, would be very useful to reflect on for anyone who is thinking about such a vehicle.

What all of this makes plain is very simply that there are many ways to achieve the true end of parental freedom through school choice without financial penalty. Increments rationally cannot be permitted to go on forever, and many dead-end detours must be avoided. Anything that ultimately maintains EFM, such as public school choice, cannot be seen as adequate. But there are *many* excellent, gradual but true, school choice methods which can make clear the light at the tunnel's end and at the same time give reassurance and confidence to those who are wary.

Letting Parents' Rights Match Their Responsibilities

The prerequisite for thinking clearly about school funding policies is to see and acknowledge that naturally and rightly we hold parents responsible for the all-around nurturing of their children. And, with relatively few dysfunctional exceptions, parents of every kind want the welfare of those children. While we want to make special provision for the welfare of the few children of dysfunctional or malevolent parents, it is a form of social insanity to design the *basic*, comprehensive funding system as if all, or most, or even many parents were indifferent to the child's welfare. Yet that is precisely what EFM does. It puts financial obstacles between parents' love and responsibilities, on the one hand; and the rights and capabilities of those parents, on the other. It imposes on them a severe financial penalty if they want to choose the school they judge best for their sons and daughters. That is wrong, it is unbalanced, and it is unnatural.

School choice will restore the natural order of things by removing the artificial impediment of financial penalty. It will once again enable parents to follow their best loving, caring instincts in selecting the educational environment for their youngsters. That is intrinsic to school choice, just as parental frustration and obstruction are intrinsic to EFM's self-protective tendencies.

But we are not dealing just with essences and abstractions—"My, isn't school choice lovely to contemplate?" Yes, it is. That is where we want to go, where schools are seen as means to the end of children's education, not as ends in themselves; where they exist to serve, rather than be served; and where parents judge how well they are serving. The consistency with which public opinion polls show school choice in the abstract is supported by citizens in general shows its logical power and compellingness.

But the harder question is not where we want to go, but how to get there from here? How to organize, how to root out the entrenched opposition, how to dispel the smoke screens so the uninitiated and the "altruistic corollaries" can see clearly, how to relate to the political process, and how in each state to shape a winning proposal to begin the process of fundamental change?

Even though the effort to free America's parents, by Herculean exertions, has managed to get school choice started; even though a beginning has been made to lift the oppressive inertia manipulated by the defenders of the status quo; America's school choice advocates should not stop until they have achieved something like a Danish or Australian North Star condition. Those and other societies have created essentially ideal parental choice policies through which parental freedom is made equivalent to parental responsibilities. That should be the ultimate objective in all American jurisdictions. There is literally *no* objective reason for settling for less, as I hope this book has helped make plain. When the citizens of the fifty states get to that objective, I urge them to enjoy the moment, for it will not then be long until today's educational finance monopoly status quo seems to be only an unlikely nightmare. And the following generation will not be able to imagine, any more than today's Danes, Dutch, or Australians can imagine, why any society would impose on itself the kind of parental dislocations and injustices which come inevitably from educational finance monopoly.

Index